Table of Contents

Chapter 1: Understanding Heart Health and Nutrition 3

    1.1. The Science of Heart Health 3

    1.2. Building a Heart-Healthy Pantry 4

    1.3. Meal Planning for a Busy Family 6

Chapter 2: Quick and Easy Cooking Techniques 7

    2.1. Healthy Cooking Methods 7

    2.2. Time-Saving Tips for Busy Parents 8

    2.3. Smart Tools for Heart-Healthy Cooking 10

Chapter 3: 101 Heart-Healthy Recipes 11

    3.1 Breakfast 11

    3.2 Lunch 21

    3.3 Dinner 31

    3.4 Snacks 41

    3.5 Desserts 51

    3.6 Beverages 59

Chapter 4: Staying Committed to Heart Health 64

Ingredient Index 68

Vegan Substitutes 70

Bio Author 71

CHAPTER 1: UNDERSTANDING HEART HEALTH AND NUTRITION

1.1. The Science of Heart Health

Your heart works tirelessly, pumping blood throughout your body to deliver oxygen and nutrients to every cell. This essential organ depends on a balanced diet to function optimally. Poor dietary choices can damage blood vessels, increase blood pressure, and elevate cholesterol levels, all of which contribute to heart disease. On the other hand, a nutrient-dense, heart-healthy diet can help prevent, manage, and even reverse certain cardiovascular conditions.

How Diet Affects the Heart

The relationship between diet and heart health is complex but incredibly impactful. A diet rich in highly processed foods, saturated fats, and added sugars can lead to **chronic inflammation**, which plays a significant role in the development of heart disease. Chronic inflammation damages the arteries and promotes the formation of plaque, which hardens and narrows the arteries, leading to **atherosclerosis**.

In contrast, a diet focused on whole foods—like fruits, vegetables, lean proteins, and healthy fats—supports cardiovascular function by reducing inflammation, improving blood lipid levels, and regulating blood pressure.

Key Nutrients for a Healthy Heart

Certain nutrients are proven to protect and nourish the heart. Prioritizing these can make a significant difference in heart health.

- **Omega-3 Fatty Acids**: Omega-3s are crucial for heart health due to their anti-inflammatory properties and ability to lower triglycerides. They are predominantly found in fatty fish like salmon, mackerel, and sardines, but can also be sourced from flaxseeds, chia seeds, and walnuts. Studies suggest that consuming 1-2 servings of fish per week (around 8 oz or 225 grams) can reduce the risk of heart disease. If fish isn't a regular part of your diet, consider high-quality omega-3 supplements like fish oil or algae oil.

- **Fiber**: Soluble fiber, found in foods like oats, beans, lentils, and certain fruits, has been shown to lower LDL cholesterol by binding to cholesterol molecules in the digestive tract, preventing their absorption. In addition, fiber-rich foods help regulate blood sugar levels, which can reduce the risk of developing diabetes—a significant risk factor for heart disease. Aim for at least 25-30 grams of fiber per day.

- **Potassium**: This electrolyte helps maintain normal blood pressure by balancing the effects of sodium. Potassium-rich foods like bananas, avocados, sweet potatoes, and spinach should be incorporated regularly. It's recommended that adults consume 2,300-3,400 milligrams of potassium daily, depending on individual needs.

- **Antioxidants**: These compounds help neutralize free radicals, which are harmful molecules that cause oxidative stress and damage cells, including those in your cardiovascular system. Foods like berries, dark chocolate, leafy greens, and nuts are high in antioxidants, including vitamin C, vitamin E, and flavonoids, which support heart health by protecting blood vessels from damage.

- **Magnesium**: Magnesium plays a vital role in regulating heart rhythm and blood pressure. This mineral is often deficient in many people's diets, but it can be found in foods like dark leafy greens, nuts, seeds, and whole grains. Ensuring you get enough magnesium can also help reduce muscle cramps and improve energy levels, making it easier to stay active—a critical factor in heart health.

- **Polyphenols**: Found in foods like olive oil, tea, dark chocolate, and red wine (in moderation), polyphenols are plant compounds with powerful anti-inflammatory and antioxidant effects. They support vascular health by improving endothelial function (the lining of the blood vessels) and reducing blood pressure.

The Role of Cholesterol and Blood Pressure

Managing cholesterol and blood pressure is crucial in maintaining heart health, and diet plays an integral role in both.

- **Cholesterol**: There are two main types of cholesterol that we focus on:
  - **LDL (Low-Density Lipoprotein)**, or "bad" cholesterol, contributes to plaque buildup in the arteries. High levels of LDL increase your risk of heart disease.
  - **HDL (High-Density Lipoprotein)**, or "good" cholesterol, helps transport LDL away from the arteries and back to the liver for elimination. Higher levels of HDL are protective against heart disease.

You can improve cholesterol levels by:

- Reducing saturated fat intake (found in red meat, butter, and full-fat dairy).
- Eliminating trans fats from processed foods.
- Increasing fiber intake and consuming foods like oats, flaxseeds, and nuts.
- Choosing healthier fats such as olive oil and avocados.

- **Blood Pressure**: Elevated blood pressure, or **hypertension**, puts extra strain on your heart and blood vessels, increasing the risk of heart attacks and strokes. Sodium intake is directly linked to blood pressure, with excess salt causing the body to retain water, increasing blood volume and pressure. To manage blood pressure:
  - Limit sodium intake to less than 2,300 milligrams per day (about 1 teaspoon of salt), but aim for 1,500 milligrams if you're at risk for hypertension.
  - Increase potassium-rich foods, as potassium helps counteract sodium's effects and relaxes blood vessels.
  - Focus on foods rich in magnesium, which helps regulate blood pressure.

1.2. Building a Heart-Healthy Pantry

The secret to consistently eating well is having a pantry stocked with heart-healthy ingredients. When your kitchen is filled with wholesome foods, it becomes easier to prepare meals that are both delicious and nutritious.

Essential Heart-Healthy Ingredients

These are the core items you should always have in your pantry, fridge, and freezer to make heart-healthy meals quickly and easily:

- **Whole Grains**: Whole grains like brown rice, quinoa, oats, and whole wheat pasta are rich in fiber and B vitamins. Unlike refined grains, whole grains help reduce cholesterol and regulate blood sugar.

- **Legumes**: Beans, lentils, and chickpeas are nutrient powerhouses. They're high in protein and fiber while being low in fat. Use them in soups, stews, salads, and even as meat substitutes in burgers or tacos.

- **Lean Proteins**: Skinless poultry, fish, and plant-based proteins like tofu and tempeh provide essential amino acids without the high levels of saturated fats found in red meats. For vegetarians, incorporating a variety of plant-based proteins ensures a full spectrum of amino acids.

- **Healthy Fats**: Opt for unsaturated fats, such as those found in olive oil, nuts, seeds, and avocados. These fats help improve cholesterol profiles and provide anti-inflammatory benefits.

- **Frozen Vegetables and Fruits**: Frozen produce retains much of its nutrient content and is perfect for adding to smoothies, stir-fries, soups, and stews. Having them on hand makes it easier to include vegetables in every meal.

- **Herbs and Spices**: Fresh and dried herbs like basil, rosemary, turmeric, and garlic add flavor without the need for excessive salt or sugar. Many spices also have anti-inflammatory properties, making them beneficial for heart health.

Substitutes for Common Unhealthy Ingredients

Making simple swaps in your everyday cooking can have a big impact on your heart health:

- **Butter → Olive Oil**: Butter is high in saturated fats, while olive oil contains heart-healthy monounsaturated fats. Use olive oil for sautéing or as a salad dressing base.

- **White Rice → Quinoa or Brown Rice**: White rice has been stripped of its fiber and nutrients, while quinoa and brown rice provide more fiber, protein, and minerals.

- **Sour Cream → Greek Yogurt**: Greek yogurt is a great substitute for sour cream in recipes, offering protein and probiotics without the high saturated fat content.

Stocking Your Kitchen for Quick and Easy Meals

To simplify heart-healthy eating, fill your pantry with versatile, nutritious staples:

- **Canned Beans and Lentils**: Look for low-sodium options. They're perfect for soups, salads, and stews.

- **Canned Tomatoes**: Choose no-salt-added varieties to use in sauces, stews, and casseroles.

- **Whole Wheat Pasta and Grains**: Quick-cooking grains like quinoa, bulgur, and couscous can be prepared in under 15 minutes.

- **Frozen Vegetables**: These are convenient and retain most of their nutritional value, allowing you to add a serving of veggies to any meal in no time.

1.3. Meal Planning for a Busy Family

Meal planning is one of the most effective tools for ensuring that you and your family stay on track with heart-healthy eating, even during busy weeks. By planning your meals in advance, you reduce the temptation to rely on processed or fast foods, and you can save time and money.

Strategies for Meal Prep and Planning

- **Plan Your Meals Weekly**: Dedicate time each week to plan breakfasts, lunches, dinners, and snacks. Choose recipes that can be made in bulk or repurposed for multiple meals.

- **Batch Cooking**: Cook large portions of grains, proteins, or soups at once, and store them in airtight containers in the fridge or freezer for easy reheating.

- **Use Time-Saving Tools**: Slow cookers, instant pots, and pressure cookers can make meal preparation much easier. They allow you to prepare meals in advance or set them to cook while you're busy with other tasks.

How to Read Nutrition Labels

Understanding nutrition labels is key to making informed decisions about what you eat. Here are some tips:

- **Serving Size**: Be mindful of the serving size listed on the label, as all the nutritional information is based on this amount.

- **Saturated Fat**: Foods with high levels of saturated fat (more than 5 grams per serving) should be eaten in moderation, as these can raise LDL cholesterol levels.

- **Sodium**: Choose products that contain less than 140 milligrams of sodium per serving to help manage blood pressure.

- **Fiber**: Look for foods with at least 3 grams of fiber per serving, as fiber is crucial for maintaining healthy cholesterol and blood sugar levels.

Budgeting for Heart-Healthy Eating

Eating heart-healthy doesn't need to be expensive. With a few smart strategies, you can enjoy nutritious meals without breaking the bank:

- **Buy in Bulk**: Purchase grains, beans, and nuts in bulk to save money.

- **Seasonal Produce**: Opt for seasonal fruits and vegetables, as they are often less expensive and fresher.

- **Cook at Home**: Preparing meals at home allows you to control the ingredients, reduce added fats and sodium, and avoid the extra costs associated with dining out.

CHAPTER 2: QUICK AND EASY COOKING TECHNIQUES

Cooking healthy meals doesn't have to be time-consuming or complicated. In fact, with the right methods and strategies, you can prepare delicious, heart-healthy meals quickly and efficiently, even on the busiest days. In this chapter, we'll explore cooking techniques that maximize nutrition and flavor while minimizing unhealthy fats, excess calories, and sodium. We'll also share tips to help you save time and make meal prep more manageable for your family.

2.1. Healthy Cooking Methods

The way you cook your food can have a significant impact on its nutritional value and, ultimately, your heart health. By using techniques that preserve nutrients and reduce the need for unhealthy ingredients, you can create meals that are both heart-friendly and flavorful.

Steaming, Grilling, and Baking vs. Frying

- **Steaming**: One of the healthiest cooking methods, steaming involves cooking food with the steam produced by boiling water. It's ideal for vegetables, fish, and even grains. Because steaming doesn't require added fats, it helps retain the natural flavors and nutrients of the ingredients. For vegetables, steaming helps preserve water-soluble vitamins like vitamin C and folate, which can be lost in other cooking methods.

- **Grilling**: Grilling is a great way to add flavor to your food without the need for added fats. Whether you're grilling vegetables, lean meats, or fish, this method allows excess fat to drip off while keeping the food moist and delicious. However, be cautious of over-charring, as excessive grilling at high temperatures can produce harmful compounds. Keep the grill temperature moderate and cook meats to a safe internal temperature without burning.

- **Baking**: Baking allows you to prepare everything from lean proteins to whole grains and even desserts without the need for excessive oil or butter. Use this method for dishes like baked salmon, chicken breast, or roasted vegetables. Baking at lower temperatures (under 375°F or 190°C) ensures that your ingredients retain their moisture and nutrients.

- **Frying**: Although fried foods are often associated with rich flavors and crispy textures, frying adds a significant amount of unhealthy fats to your diet, particularly trans fats and saturated fats, which increase cholesterol levels and contribute to heart disease. If you're craving crispy textures, try **baking or air-frying** for similar results with much less oil.

The Benefits of Slow Cooking and Pressure Cooking

- **Slow Cooking**: Slow cookers are a fantastic tool for creating hearty, nutrient-rich meals with minimal effort. Because foods cook at low temperatures over a longer period, the natural flavors and juices are preserved without the need for added fats. This method is perfect for making soups, stews, and lean cuts of meat. The slow cooking process also allows you to batch cook meals, which can be portioned out and frozen for future use.

- **Pressure Cooking**: Pressure cookers, including Instant Pots, use steam pressure to cook food rapidly, making them perfect for busy families. This method is particularly good for preserving nutrients because the shorter cooking time reduces the loss of heat-sensitive vitamins. Pressure cooking is ideal for legumes, whole grains, and tougher cuts of lean meat that become tender in a fraction of the usual time.

Both slow cooking and pressure cooking can help you create meals rich in fiber and protein, like lentil stews, chickpea curries, or beef and vegetable soups, all of which are excellent for heart health.

Maximizing Flavor Without Extra Calories

Heart-healthy meals don't have to be bland or boring. You can easily enhance flavor without resorting to unhealthy ingredients like excessive salt, butter, or sugar. Here are some techniques to boost flavor while keeping your meals nutritious:

- **Herbs and Spices**: Fresh herbs like basil, cilantro, rosemary, and parsley, along with dried spices like turmeric, cumin, and paprika, add layers of flavor and have additional health benefits. For example, turmeric contains curcumin, a powerful anti-inflammatory compound, while garlic has been shown to lower cholesterol and reduce blood pressure.

- **Citrus**: A squeeze of lemon or lime can brighten up the flavor of a dish and reduce the need for added salt. Citrus fruits also provide vitamin C and antioxidants that support heart health.

- **Vinegars and Mustards**: Balsamic, apple cider, or red wine vinegars add tanginess and depth to salads, vegetables, and proteins. Similarly, mustard (look for varieties without added sugar) can provide a sharp, savory flavor that complements many dishes without the need for extra salt or fat.

- **Healthy Fats for Flavor**: While it's important to limit saturated and trans fats, certain unsaturated fats are both healthy and flavorful. Drizzle a small amount of extra virgin olive oil over roasted vegetables or use avocado oil for sautéing—it adds richness without compromising heart health.

2.2. Time-Saving Tips for Busy Parents

Balancing family, work, and a heart-healthy diet can be a challenge, but with a few strategic time-saving techniques, it's entirely possible to serve nutritious meals even on your busiest days.

Batch Cooking and Freezing Meals

Batch cooking is one of the best strategies for saving time and ensuring you always have healthy meals on hand. Here's how to make it work:

- **Cook in Large Quantities**: On weekends or days when you have more time, prepare large batches of staples like soups, stews, grains, and proteins. For example, a big pot of lentil soup or a tray of roasted chicken breasts can be divided into portions and stored for the week ahead.

- **Freeze in Portions**: Use airtight containers or freezer bags to store individual portions of cooked meals. This not only prevents waste but also makes it easy to reheat a single serving when you're short on time. Frozen meals can last for several months, so you can batch cook once a week or even once a month.
- **Label and Organize**: Always label your frozen meals with the name and date to keep track of what you have. This will help ensure you rotate through your meals before they lose quality.

Using Leftovers Creatively

Transforming leftovers into new meals is a great way to reduce food waste and save time. With a little creativity, you can turn last night's dinner into today's lunch:

- **Repurpose Proteins**: Grilled chicken, baked salmon, or roasted vegetables can easily be turned into new dishes. For example, leftover chicken can be shredded and used in wraps, salads, or stir-fries. Roasted vegetables can be added to a whole grain bowl or mixed into a frittata.
- **Soups and Stews**: Leftover grains, legumes, and proteins can often be repurposed into a quick soup or stew. Add a low-sodium broth, fresh or frozen vegetables, and season with herbs for a completely new meal that's hearty and satisfying.
- **Salads and Grain Bowls**: Leftover vegetables, lean proteins, and grains can quickly be transformed into hearty salads or grain bowls. Simply toss them with some leafy greens, a heart-healthy dressing (like olive oil and lemon juice), and a sprinkle of seeds or nuts for added crunch.

One-Pan and Sheet-Pan Meals for Minimal Cleanup

One-pan and sheet-pan meals are excellent for busy families because they require minimal prep and cleanup. You simply toss all your ingredients onto a baking sheet or into a pan and let the oven do the work.

- **Sheet-Pan Dinners**: Combine lean proteins like chicken breasts or fish fillets with vegetables such as broccoli, carrots, or sweet potatoes. Toss everything in a small amount of olive oil and seasoning, and roast in the oven. Within 20-30 minutes, you'll have a complete, balanced meal with minimal cleanup.
- **Stir-Fries**: Stir-fries are another quick, one-pan solution. Use a wok or large skillet to sauté lean proteins like shrimp or tofu with a variety of colorful vegetables. Serve with brown rice or quinoa for a fiber-rich, heart-healthy meal. The entire cooking process takes less than 20 minutes, and you only have one pan to clean.

2.3. Smart Tools for Heart-Healthy Cooking

Investing in a few kitchen tools can drastically reduce the time and effort needed to prepare heart-healthy meals. Here are some tools worth considering:

- **Instant Pot or Pressure Cooker**: These versatile appliances can cook grains, beans, and even meats in a fraction of the time it would take on the stovetop. Use them to make stews, soups, and even yogurt—perfect for meal prepping.

- **Slow Cooker**: Perfect for setting up meals in the morning and coming home to a fully cooked dish. The low and slow cooking process helps tenderize tough cuts of lean meat and enhances flavors without the need for extra fats.

- **High-Quality Knives**: A good set of sharp knives can speed up chopping and prepping significantly. It also makes slicing vegetables and trimming fats from proteins much easier and safer.

- **Food Processor or Blender**: Ideal for quickly preparing sauces, dips, soups, and smoothies. You can also use these appliances to make homemade nut butters or even heart-healthy desserts like avocado mousse or almond flour dough.

CHAPTER 3: 101 HEART-HEALTHY RECIPES

3.1 BREAKFAST

1. Avocado Toast with Poached Egg

 Prep.Time: 5 minutes
Cook Time: 5 minutes
Total Time: 10 minutes

 Equipment Needed: Toaster, small saucepan, slotted spoon, knife

 Difficulty: 1/5

 Ingredient List for 1 Serving:

- 1 slice whole grain bread
- 1/2 ripe avocado, mashed (about 75 g)
- 1 large egg
- 1 tablespoon lemon juice (15 ml)
- Salt and pepper to taste
- 1 teaspoon olive oil (5 ml)
- Optional: red pepper flakes or fresh herbs for garnish

Step-by-Step Instructions:

1. **Preparation:** Toast the slice of whole grain bread until golden brown.
2. **Poaching the Egg:** Bring a small saucepan of water to a simmer. Crack the egg into a small bowl, then gently slide it into the simmering water. Cook for 3-4 minutes until the egg white is set but the yolk remains runny. Remove with a slotted spoon and set aside.
3. **Assembling:** Mash the avocado with lemon juice, salt, and pepper. Spread it on the toasted bread.
4. **Serving:** Top the avocado toast with the poached egg. Optionally, sprinkle with red pepper flakes or fresh herbs.

Macronutrients:

Calories: 300 kcal | Protein: 10g | Carbohydrates: 22g | Fiber: 8g | Sugars: 2g | Total Fat: 20g | Saturated Fat: 4g | Cholesterol: 185mg | Sodium: 300mg | Potassium: 600mg

Micronutrients:

Vitamin A: 20% Daily Value | Vitamin C: 15% Daily Value | Calcium: 10% Daily Value | Iron: 15% Daily Value

2. Spinach & Feta Scramble

 Prep.Time: 5 minutes
Cook Time: 5 minutes
Total Time: 10 minutes

 Equipment Needed: Skillet, spatula, knife

 Difficulty: 1/5

 Ingredient List for 1 Serving:

- 2 large eggs
- 1/2 cup fresh spinach, chopped (120 ml, 35 g)
- 1/4 cup feta cheese, crumbled (60 ml, 30 g)
- 1 tablespoon olive oil (15 ml)
- 1/4 teaspoon salt (1.5 g)
- 1/4 teaspoon black pepper (1 g)

Step-by-Step Instructions:

1. **Preparation:** Heat olive oil in a skillet over medium heat. Add chopped spinach and sauté until wilted. Set aside.
2. **Cooking:** Whisk eggs with salt and pepper. Pour into the skillet and scramble until cooked through.
3. **Adding:** Stir in the feta cheese and cooked spinach.
4. **Assembling:** Serve the scramble hot.

Macronutrients:

Calories: 330 kcal | Protein: 18g | Carbohydrates: 5g | Fiber: 2g | Sugars: 2g | Total Fat: 27g | Saturated Fat: 9g | Cholesterol: 425mg | Sodium: 680mg | Potassium: 400mg

Micronutrients:

Vitamin A: 60% Daily Value | Vitamin C: 15% Daily Value | Calcium: 20% Daily Value | Iron: 15% Daily Value

3. Quinoa Porridge with Mixed Berries

 Prep.Time: 5 minutes
Cook Time: 15 minutes
Total Time: 20 minutes

 Equipment Needed: Saucepan, spoon, measuring cups

 Difficulty: 2/5

 Ingredient List for 1 Serving:
- 1/4 cup quinoa, rinsed (45 g)
- 3/4 cup water or almond milk (180 ml)
- 1/4 teaspoon cinnamon (1 g)
- 1/4 cup mixed berries (40 g)
- 1 tablespoon honey or maple syrup (15 ml)
- 1 tablespoon chia seeds (10 g)

Step-by-Step Instructions:

1. **Cooking Quinoa:** In a saucepan, combine quinoa, water (or almond milk), and cinnamon. Bring to a boil, then reduce to a simmer. Cook for about 15 minutes, or until the quinoa has absorbed the liquid and becomes soft.
2. **Topping:** Once cooked, stir in chia seeds and allow the porridge to thicken slightly.
3. **Assembling:** Serve the porridge in a bowl and top with mixed berries and honey or maple syrup, if desired.

Macronutrients:
Calories: 250 kcal | Protein: 7g | Carbohydrates: 42g | Fiber: 6g | Sugars: 12g | Total Fat: 6g | Saturated Fat: 1g | Cholesterol: 0mg | Sodium: 15mg | Potassium: 300mg

Micronutrients:
Vitamin A: 2% Daily Value | Vitamin C: 20% Daily Value | Calcium: 10% Daily Value | Iron: 10% Daily Value

4. Oatmeal Pancakes with Fresh Fruit

 Prep.Time: 10 minutes
Cook Time: 10 minutes
Total Time: 20 minutes

 Equipment Needed: Mixing bowl, non-stick skillet, spatula

 Difficulty: 2/5

 Ingredient List for 1 Serving:
- 1/2 cup rolled oats (45 g)
- 1/4 cup almond milk or milk of choice (60 ml)
- 1 egg
- 1/2 teaspoon baking powder (2 g)
- 1/2 teaspoon vanilla extract (2 ml)
- 1/4 cup fresh fruit (50 g)
- 1 tablespoon maple syrup (15 ml, optional)

Step-by-Step Instructions:

1. **Mixing:** In a mixing bowl, combine oats, almond milk, egg, baking powder, and vanilla extract. Stir until well combined and let sit for 5 minutes.
2. **Cooking:** Heat a non-stick skillet over medium heat. Pour small amounts of batter into the skillet to form pancakes. Cook for about 2-3 minutes per side or until golden brown.
3. **Serving:** Top pancakes with fresh fruit and drizzle with maple syrup if desired.

Macronutrients:
Calories: 350 kcal | Protein: 10g | Carbohydrates: 55g | Fiber: 8g | Sugars: 12g | Total Fat: 8g | Saturated Fat: 1g | Cholesterol: 185mg | Sodium: 200mg | Potassium: 300mg

Micronutrients:
Vitamin A: 4% Daily Value | Vitamin C: 10% Daily Value | Calcium: 15% Daily Value | Iron: 15% Daily Value

5. Chia Seed Pudding with Almond Milk

 Prep.Time: 5 minutes
Set Time: 2 hours or overnight

 Equipment Needed: Mixing bowl, whisk, fridge

 Difficulty: 1/5

 Ingredient List for 1 Serving:
- 1/4 cup chia seeds (40 g)
- 1 cup unsweetened almond milk (240 ml)
- 1 tablespoon honey or maple syrup (15 ml)
- 1/4 teaspoon vanilla extract (1 ml)
- Fresh berries or nuts for topping

Step-by-Step Instructions:
1. **Mixing:** In a bowl, whisk together chia seeds, almond milk, honey (or maple syrup), and vanilla extract.
2. **Setting:** Cover and refrigerate for at least 2 hours or overnight. The chia seeds will absorb the liquid and thicken into a pudding-like consistency.
3. **Serving:** Stir the pudding and top with fresh berries or nuts before serving.

Macronutrients:
Calories: 220 kcal | Protein: 6g | Carbohydrates: 20g | Fiber: 10g | Sugars: 10g | Total Fat: 12g | Saturated Fat: 1g | Cholesterol: 0mg | Sodium: 100mg | Potassium: 250mg

Micronutrients:
Vitamin A: 2% Daily Value | Vitamin C: 10% Daily Value | Calcium: 30% Daily Value | Iron: 15% Daily Value

6. Whole Grain Banana Nut Bread (Slice)

 Prep.Time: 10 minutes
Cook Time: 50 minutes
Total Time: 1 hours

 Equipment Needed: Mixing bowl, loaf pan, oven

 Difficulty: 2/5

 Ingredient List for 10 Slices:
- 1 1/2 cups whole wheat flour (180 g)
- 1/2 cup mashed ripe bananas (120 g, about 1 large banana)
- 1/4 cup honey or maple syrup (60 ml)
- 1/4 cup olive oil (60 ml)
- 2 large eggs
- 1 teaspoon baking soda (5 g)
- 1/4 teaspoon salt (1.5 g)
- 1/2 teaspoon cinnamon (2 g)
- 1/4 cup chopped walnuts (30 g)

Step-by-Step Instructions:
1. **Preparation:** Preheat the oven to 350°F (175°C). Grease a loaf pan with a little oil or line it with parchment paper.
2. **Mixing:** In a large bowl, mix the mashed bananas, honey (or maple syrup), olive oil, and eggs until smooth. In a separate bowl, combine whole wheat flour, baking soda, salt, and cinnamon.
3. **Baking:** Slowly add the dry ingredients to the wet ingredients and stir until combined. Fold in the chopped walnuts. Pour the batter into the loaf pan and bake for 45-50 minutes, or until a toothpick inserted into the center comes out clean.
4. **Serving:** Let cool before slicing. Serve warm or at room temperature.

Macronutrients:
Calories: 180 kcal | Protein: 4g | Carbohydrates: 20g | Fiber: 3g | Sugars: 10g | Total Fat: 9g | Saturated Fat: 1g | Cholesterol: 35mg | Sodium: 150mg | Potassium: 125mg | Vitamin A: 2% Daily Value

Micronutrients:
Vitamin C: 4% Daily Value | Calcium: 2% Daily Value | Iron: 6% Daily Value

7. Kale and Mushroom Frittata

 Prep.Time: 10 minutes
Cook Time: 15 minutes
Total Time: 25 minutes

 Equipment Needed: Skillet, whisk, spatula

 Difficulty: 2/5

 Ingredient List for 1 Serving:
- 4 large eggs
- 1/2 cup chopped kale (120 ml, 20 g)
- 1/2 cup sliced mushrooms (120 ml, 40 g)
- 1/4 cup feta cheese, crumbled (60 ml, 30 g)
- 1 tablespoon olive oil (15 ml)
- Salt and pepper to taste

Step-by-Step Instructions:

1. **Preparation:** Heat olive oil in a medium skillet over medium heat. Add the mushrooms and sauté until softened, about 5 minutes. Stir in the kale and cook for another 2-3 minutes until wilted. Set aside.
2. **Cooking:** In a bowl, whisk the eggs with a pinch of salt and pepper. Pour the eggs into the skillet and cook for 5-6 minutes until mostly set.
3. **Adding:** Sprinkle the feta cheese over the top and transfer the skillet to the oven under a broiler for 2-3 minutes, or until the top is golden and fully set.
4. **Serving:** Slice the frittata into wedges and serve warm.

Macronutrients:
Calories: 250 kcal | Protein: 15g | Carbohydrates: 5g | Fiber: 2g | Sugars: 2g | Total Fat: 20g | Saturated Fat: 6g | Cholesterol: 380mg | Sodium: 450mg | Potassium: 400mg

Micronutrients:
Vitamin A: 50% Daily Value | Vitamin C: 20% Daily Value | Calcium: 15% Daily Value | Iron: 10% Daily Value

8. Berry and Flaxseed Smoothie

 Prep.Time: 5 minutes
Total Time: 5 minutes

 Equipment Needed: Bowl, spoon

 Difficulty: 1/5

 Ingredient List for 1 Serving:
- 1/2 cup mixed berries (120 ml, 75 g)
- 1/2 banana
- 1 tablespoon flaxseeds (15 g)
- 1 cup unsweetened almond milk (240 ml)
- 1/4 teaspoon cinnamon (1 g)

Step-by-Step Instructions:

1. **Blending:** Add the mixed berries, banana, flaxseeds, almond milk, and cinnamon to a blender.
2. **Mixing:** Blend on high speed until smooth and creamy.
3. **Serving:** Pour into a glass and enjoy immediately.

Macronutrients:
Calories: 300 kcal | Protein: 5g | Carbohydrates: 40g | Fiber: 10g | Sugars: 15g | Total Fat: 12g | Saturated Fat: 1g | Cholesterol: 0mg | Sodium: 180mg | Potassium: 450mg

Micronutrients:
Vitamin A: 10% Daily Value | Vitamin C: 60% Daily Value | Calcium: 30% Daily Value | Iron: 8% Daily Value

9. Sweet Potato and Black Bean Breakfast Burrito

Prep.Time: 5 minutes
Cook Time: 15 minutes
Total Time: 25 minutes

Equipment Needed: Blender

Difficulty: 3/5

Ingredient List for 1 Serving:
- 1 small sweet potato, peeled and diced (about 150 g)
- 1/4 cup black beans (60 ml, 40 g), cooked
- 1 large egg
- 1/4 cup shredded cheddar cheese (60 ml, 30 g)
- 1 tablespoon olive oil (15 ml)
- 1 whole wheat tortilla (10-inch, 25 cm)
- Salt and pepper to taste

Step-by-Step Instructions:
1. **Cooking:** Heat olive oil in a skillet over medium heat. Add the diced sweet potato and sauté for about 10 minutes until tender. Stir in the black beans and cook for another 2-3 minutes.
2. **Eggs:** In a separate pan, scramble the egg with a pinch of salt and pepper.
3. **Assembling:** Warm the tortilla in the microwave or on the stovetop. Fill it with the sweet potato mixture, scrambled egg, and shredded cheese. Roll up the burrito and serve warm.

Macronutrients:

Calories: 400 kcal | Protein: 18g | Carbohydrates: 45g | Fiber: 8g | Sugars: 7g | Total Fat: 20g | Saturated Fat: 6g | Cholesterol: 210mg | Sodium: 480mg | Potassium: 550mg | Vitamin A: 120% Daily Value

Micronutrients:

Vitamin C: 15% Daily Value | Calcium: 25% Daily Value | Iron: 15% Daily Value

10. Greek Yogurt Parfait with Granola and Honey

Prep.Time: 5 minutes
Total Time: 5 minutes

Equipment Needed: Mixing bowl, spoon

Difficulty: 2/5

Ingredient List for 1 Serving:
- 1/2 cup Greek yogurt (120 ml, 125 g)
- 1/4 cup granola (60 ml, 30 g)
- 1 tablespoon honey (15 ml)
- 1/4 cup mixed berries (60 ml, 40 g)

Step-by-Step Instructions:
1. **Layering:** In a serving glass or bowl, layer the Greek yogurt, granola, and mixed berries.
2. **Finishing:** Drizzle honey over the top.
3. **Serving:** Serve immediately or refrigerate for up to 30 minutes.

Macronutrients:

Calories: 280 kcal | Protein: 12g | Carbohydrates: 40g | Fiber: 4g | Sugars: 18g | Total Fat: 8g | Saturated Fat: 3g | Cholesterol: 15mg | Sodium: 90mg | Potassium: 250mg | Vitamin A: 2% Daily Value

Micronutrients:

Vitamin C: 10% Daily Value | Calcium: 15% Daily Value | Iron: 6% Daily Value

11. Whole Grain Toast with Almond Butter and Berries

Prep. Time: 5 minutes
Total Time: 5 minutes

Equipment Needed: Toaster, knife

Difficulty: 1/5

Ingredient List for 1 Serving:
- 1 slice whole grain bread
- 1 tablespoon almond butter (15 ml, 16 g)
- 1/4 cup mixed berries (60 ml, 40 g)
- Optional: drizzle of honey (5 ml)

Step-by-Step Instructions:
1. **Preparation:** Toast the whole grain bread until golden brown.
2. **Assembling:** Spread the almond butter over the toast and top with mixed berries.
3. **Finishing:** Drizzle with honey if desired.

Macronutrients:
Calories: 320 kcal | Protein: 8g | Carbohydrates: 35g | Fiber: 7g | Sugars: 12g | Total Fat: 18g | Saturated Fat: 2g | Cholesterol: 0mg | Sodium: 120mg | Potassium: 350mg | Vitamin A: 2% Daily Value

Micronutrients:
Vitamin C: 15% Daily Value | Calcium: 8% Daily Value | Iron: 10% Daily Value

12. Oatmeal Porridge with Apple and Cinnamon

Prep. Time: 5 minutes
Cook Time: 10 minutes
Total Time: 15 minutes

Equipment Needed: Saucepan, spoon

Difficulty: 1/5

Ingredient List for 1 Serving:
- 1/2 cup rolled oats (45 g)
- 1 cup water or almond milk (240 ml)
- 1/2 apple, diced (about 60 g)
- 1/4 teaspoon cinnamon (1 g)
- 1 tablespoon maple syrup (15 ml)

Step-by-Step Instructions:
1. **Cooking:** In a saucepan, combine oats and water (or almond milk) and bring to a simmer. Cook for about 5-7 minutes until thickened.
2. **Adding:** Stir in the diced apple, cinnamon, and maple syrup. Cook for an additional 2-3 minutes.
3. **Serving:** Serve hot and top with more apple slices or a sprinkle of cinnamon if desired.

Macronutrients:
Calories: 250 kcal | Protein: 5g | Carbohydrates: 50g | Fiber: 6g | Sugars: 18g | Total Fat: 3g | Saturated Fat: 0.5g | Cholesterol: 0mg | Sodium: 10mg | Potassium: 220mg | Vitamin A: 1% Daily Value

Micronutrients:
Vitamin C: 6% Daily Value | Calcium: 6% Daily Value | Iron: 10% Daily Value

13. Spinach, Avocado, and Mango Smoothie

Prep.Time: 5 minutes
Total Time: 5 minutes

Equipment Needed: Blender, bowl

Difficulty: 1/5

Ingredient List for 1 Serving:
- 1 scoop plant-based protein powder
- 1/2 cup unsweetened almond milk
- 1/4 avocado
- 1/4 cup spinach
- 1/4 cup mixed berries
- 1 tablespoon chia seeds

🏆 Step-by-Step Instructions:
1. **Blending:** In a blender, combine protein powder, almond milk, avocado, spinach, and berries. Blend until smooth.
2. **Pouring:** Pour the smoothie into a bowl.
3. **Topping:** Sprinkle chia seeds on top and add extra berries or nuts if desired.
4. **Serving:** Serve immediately.

🍽 Macronutrients:
Calories: 280 kcal | Protein: 5g | Carbohydrates: 35g | Fiber: 10g | Sugars: 15g | Total Fat: 14g | Saturated Fat: 2g | Cholesterol: 0mg | Sodium: 25mg | Potassium: 500mg | Vitamin A: 50% Daily Value

🔬 Micronutrients:
Vitamin C: 90% Daily Value | Calcium: 10% Daily Value | Iron: 15% Daily Value

14. Buckwheat Pancakes with Maple Syrup and Nuts

Prep.Time: 10 minutes
Cook Time: 10 minutes
Total Time: 20 minutes

Equipment Needed: Mixing bowl, non-stick skillet, spatula

Difficulty: 2/5

Ingredient List for 1 Serving:
- 1/2 cup buckwheat flour (60 g)
- 1/2 teaspoon baking powder (2 g)
- 1/2 cup almond milk or milk of choice (120 ml)
- 1 large egg
- 1 tablespoon maple syrup (15 ml)
- 1 tablespoon chopped nuts (15 g)
- 1 tablespoon olive oil (15 ml)

🏆 Step-by-Step Instructions:
1. **Mixing:** In a mixing bowl, combine buckwheat flour and baking powder. Whisk in the milk and egg until smooth.
2. **Cooking:** Heat olive oil in a non-stick skillet over medium heat. Pour small amounts of batter into the skillet to form pancakes. Cook for 2-3 minutes per side until golden brown.
3. **Serving:** Serve pancakes drizzled with maple syrup and topped with chopped nuts.

🍽 Macronutrients:
Calories: 370 kcal | Protein: 12g | Carbohydrates: 50g | Fiber: 5g | Sugars: 12g | Total Fat: 14g | Saturated Fat: 2g | Cholesterol: 185mg | Sodium: 200mg | Potassium: 350mg

🔬 Micronutrients:
Vitamin A: 4% Daily Value | Vitamin C: 0% Daily Value | Calcium: 15% Daily Value | Iron: 20% Daily Value

15. Greek Yogurt with Honey, Nuts, and Chia Seeds

Prep.Time: 5 minutes
Total Time: 5 minutes

Equipment Needed: Spoon, mixing bowl

Difficulty: 1/5

Ingredient List for 1 Serving:
- 1/2 cup Greek yogurt (120 ml, 125 g)
- 1 tablespoon honey (15 ml)
- 1 tablespoon chia seeds (10 g)
- 1 tablespoon chopped nuts (15 g)

Step-by-Step Instructions:
1. **Mixing:** In a mixing bowl, stir together Greek yogurt, honey, chia seeds, and chopped nuts.
2. **Serving:** Serve immediately or refrigerate for up to 1 hour to allow the chia seeds to soften.

Macronutrients:
Calories: 290 kcal | Protein: 12g | Carbohydrates: 25g | Fiber: 5g | Sugars: 18g | Total Fat: 15g | Saturated Fat: 3g | Cholesterol: 10mg | Sodium: 75mg | Potassium: 200mg

Micronutrients:
Vitamin A: 2% Daily Value | Vitamin C: 1% Daily Value | Calcium: 15% Daily Value | Iron: 6% Daily Value

16. Whole Wheat Crepes with Ricotta and Berries

Prep.Time: 10 minutes
Cook Time: 10 minutes
Total Time: 20 minutes

Equipment Needed: Mixing bowl, non-stick skillet, spatula

Difficulty: 3/5

Ingredient List for 1 Serving:
- 1/2 cup whole wheat flour (60 g)
- 1/2 cup almond milk or milk of choice (120 ml)
- 1 large egg
- 1 tablespoon olive oil (15 ml)
- 1/4 cup ricotta cheese (60 ml, 60 g)
- 1/4 cup mixed berries (60 ml, 40 g)

Step-by-Step Instructions:
1. **Mixing:** In a mixing bowl, whisk together whole wheat flour, milk, egg, and olive oil until smooth.
2. **Cooking:** Heat a non-stick skillet over medium heat. Pour a small amount of batter into the skillet, swirling it around to form a thin crepe. Cook for about 1-2 minutes on each side.
3. **Filling:** Spread ricotta cheese over the crepe and top with mixed berries. Fold or roll the crepe and serve.

Macronutrients:
Calories: 300 kcal | Protein: 12g | Carbohydrates: 35g | Fiber: 5g | Sugars: 10g | Total Fat: 12g | Saturated Fat: 3g | Cholesterol: 185mg | Sodium: 150mg | Potassium: 350mg

Micronutrients:
Vitamin A: 4% Daily Value | Vitamin C: 10% Daily Value | Calcium: 15% Daily Value | Iron: 10% Daily Value

17. Hummus, Tomato, and Spinach Toast

Prep.Time: 5 minutes
Total Time: 5 minutes

Equipment Needed: Toaster, knife

Difficulty: 1/5

Ingredient List for 1 Serving:
- 1 slice whole grain bread
- 2 tablespoons hummus (30 ml, 30 g)
- 1/4 cup fresh spinach (60 ml, 20 g)
- 2 slices tomato

Step-by-Step Instructions:
1. **Preparation:** Toast the whole grain bread until golden brown.
2. **Assembling:** Spread the hummus over the toast, then top with spinach and tomato slices.
3. **Serving:** Serve immediately.

Macronutrients:
Calories: 230 kcal | Protein: 8g | Carbohydrates: 30g | Fiber: 7g | Sugars: 4g | Total Fat: 10g | Saturated Fat: 1g | Cholesterol: 0mg | Sodium: 250mg | Potassium: 350mg

Micronutrients:
Vitamin A: 30% Daily Value | Vitamin C: 15% Daily Value | Calcium: 8% Daily Value | Iron: 10% Daily Value

18. Egg White Omelette with Spinach and Tomatoes

Prep.Time: 5 minutes
Cook Time: 5 minutes
Total Time: 10 minutes

Equipment Needed: Skillet, spatula

Difficulty: 2/5

Ingredient List for 1 Serving:
- 3 large egg whites
- 1/4 cup fresh spinach (60 ml, 20 g)
- 1/4 cup diced tomatoes (60 ml, 40 g)
- 1 tablespoon olive oil (15 ml)
- Salt and pepper to taste

Step-by-Step Instructions:
1. **Cooking:** Heat olive oil in a skillet over medium heat. Add spinach and diced tomatoes and sauté for 2-3 minutes until wilted.
2. **Egg Whites:** In a bowl, whisk the egg whites with a pinch of salt and pepper. Pour the egg whites over the spinach and tomatoes and cook for 3-4 minutes until set.
3. **Serving:** Fold the omelette and serve warm.

Macronutrients:
Calories: 200 kcal | Protein: 15g | Carbohydrates: 4g | Fiber: 2g | Sugars: 2g | Total Fat: 14g | Saturated Fat: 2g | Cholesterol: 0mg | Sodium: 150mg | Potassium: 300mg

Micronutrients:
Vitamin A: 20% Daily Value | Vitamin C: 10% Daily Value | Calcium: 4% Daily Value | Iron: 8% Daily Value

19. Ricotta and Lemon Pancakes with Blueberries

 Prep.Time: 10 minutes
Cook Time: 10 minutes
Total Time: 20 minutes

 Equipment Needed: Mixing bowl, non-stick skillet, spatula

 Difficulty: 3/5

 Ingredient List for 1 Serving:
- 1/2 cup ricotta cheese (120 ml, 120 g)
- 1/4 cup whole wheat flour (30 g)
- 1 large egg
- 1 tablespoon lemon juice (15 ml)
- 1/2 teaspoon lemon zest (1 g)
- 1 tablespoon olive oil (15 ml)
- 1/4 cup blueberries (60 ml, 40 g)

Step-by-Step Instructions:
1. **Mixing:** In a bowl, whisk together ricotta, flour, egg, lemon juice, and lemon zest until smooth.
2. **Cooking:** Heat olive oil in a non-stick skillet over medium heat. Pour small amounts of batter into the skillet to form pancakes. Cook for 2-3 minutes per side until golden brown.
3. **Serving:** Serve the pancakes topped with fresh blueberries.

Macronutrients:
Calories: 350 kcal | Protein: 14g | Carbohydrates: 35g | Fiber: 5g | Sugars: 12g | Total Fat: 18g | Saturated Fat: 4g | Cholesterol: 185mg | Sodium: 150mg | Potassium: 250mg

Micronutrients:
Vitamin A: 8% Daily Value | Vitamin C: 15% Daily Value | Calcium: 20% Daily Value | Iron: 10% Daily Value

20. Acai Smoothie Bowl with Banana and Nuts

 Prep.Time: 5 minutes
Total Time: 5 minutes

 Equipment Needed: Blender, bowl

 Difficulty: 1/5

 Ingredient List for 2 Servings:
- 1 packet frozen acai puree (100 g)
- 1/2 banana, sliced
- 1/4 cup unsweetened almond milk (60 ml)
- 1 tablespoon chia seeds (10 g)
- 1 tablespoon chopped nuts (15 g)

Step-by-Step Instructions:
1. **Blending:** Blend acai puree, half the banana, and almond milk until smooth. Pour into a bowl.
2. **Topping:** Top with the remaining banana slices, chia seeds, and chopped nuts.
3. **Serving:** Serve immediately and enjoy as a refreshing breakfast or snack.

Macronutrients:
Calories: 330 kcal | Protein: 6g | Carbohydrates: 40g | Fiber: 8g | Sugars: 18g | Total Fat: 15g | Saturated Fat: 2g | Cholesterol: 0mg | Sodium: 30mg | Potassium: 450mg

 Micronutrients:
Vitamin A: 2% Daily Value | Vitamin C: 10% Daily Value | Calcium: 15% Daily Value | Iron: 10% Daily Value

3.2 LUNCH

21. Quinoa Salad with Chickpeas and Veggies

Prep.Time: 10 minutes
Cook Time: 15 minutes
Total Time: 25 minutes

Equipment Needed: Saucepan, mixing bowl

Difficulty: 2/5

Ingredient List for 1 Serving:
- 1/2 cup quinoa, rinsed (90 g)
- 1 cup water (240 ml)
- 1/2 cup cooked chickpeas (120 ml, 80 g)
- 1/4 cup diced cucumber (60 ml, 40 g)
- 1/4 cup cherry tomatoes, halved (60 ml, 40 g)
- 1 tablespoon olive oil (15 ml)
- 1 tablespoon lemon juice (15 ml)
- Salt and pepper to taste

Step-by-Step Instructions:
1. **Cooking Quinoa:** Bring quinoa and water to a boil, then reduce to a simmer. Cook for 15 minutes, or until quinoa is tender and water is absorbed. Let it cool.
2. **Mixing:** In a bowl, combine cooked quinoa, chickpeas, cucumber, and cherry tomatoes. Drizzle with olive oil and lemon juice. Season with salt and pepper.
3. **Serving:** Toss and serve chilled or at room temperature.

Macronutrients:
Calories: 350 kcal | Protein: 10g | Carbohydrates: 45g | Fiber: 8g | Sugars: 5g | Total Fat: 12g | Saturated Fat: 1.5g | Cholesterol: 0mg | Sodium: 220mg | Potassium: 450mg

Micronutrients:
Vitamin A: 10% Daily Value | Vitamin C: 15% Daily Value | Calcium: 6% Daily Value | Iron: 15% Daily Value

22. Grilled Chicken Caesar Wrap

Prep.Time: 10 minutes
Cook Time: 10 minutes
Total Time: 20 minutes

Equipment Needed: Grill or skillet, mixing bowl

Difficulty: 2/5

Ingredient List for 1 Serving:
- 1 small chicken breast (100 g)
- 1 whole wheat tortilla (10-inch, 25 cm)
- 1/4 cup romaine lettuce, chopped (60 ml, 20 g)
- 1 tablespoon grated Parmesan cheese (15 ml, 10 g)
- 2 tablespoons Greek yogurt (30 ml, 30 g)
- 1 teaspoon lemon juice (5 ml)
- 1/2 teaspoon Dijon mustard (2.5 ml)
- 1 teaspoon olive oil (5 ml)

Step-by-Step Instructions:
1. **Grilling Chicken:** Season the chicken breast with salt and pepper. Grill or cook in a skillet over medium heat for 4-5 minutes per side until fully cooked. Slice thinly.
2. **Making Dressing:** In a bowl, whisk together Greek yogurt, lemon juice, Dijon mustard, and olive oil.
3. **Assembling Wrap:** Spread the yogurt dressing on the tortilla, then layer with lettuce, Parmesan cheese, and sliced chicken. Roll up the wrap and serve.

Macronutrients:
Calories: 450 kcal | Protein: 35g | Carbohydrates: 40g | Fiber: 6g | Sugars: 5g | Total Fat: 18g | Saturated Fat: 5g | Cholesterol: 75mg | Sodium: 550mg | Potassium: 550mg

Micronutrients:
Vitamin A: 35% Daily Value | Vitamin C: 10% Daily Value | Calcium: 15% Daily Value | Iron: 10% Daily Value

23. Lentil Soup with Kale and Carrots

Prep.Time: 10 minutes
Cook Time: 30 minutes
Total Time: 40 minutes

Equipment Needed: Large pot, spoon

Difficulty: 2/5

Ingredient List for 1 Serving:
- 1/2 cup dried lentils (90 g)
- 4 cups vegetable broth (960 ml)
- 1/2 cup chopped kale (120 ml, 20 g)
- 1/2 cup diced carrots (120 ml, 60 g)
- 1/4 cup diced onions (60 ml, 40 g)
- 1 tablespoon olive oil (15 ml)
- 1/2 teaspoon cumin (2 g)
- Salt and pepper to taste

Step-by-Step Instructions:
1. **Sautéing Veggies:** Heat olive oil in a large pot. Add onions and carrots and sauté for 5 minutes until softened.
2. **Cooking Lentils:** Add lentils, broth, and cumin to the pot. Bring to a boil, then reduce heat and simmer for 25-30 minutes until lentils are tender.
3. **Finishing:** Stir in the chopped kale and cook for an additional 5 minutes. Season with salt and pepper.
4. **Serving:** Serve hot with a drizzle of olive oil if desired.

Macronutrients:

Calories: 220 kcal | Protein: 12g | Carbohydrates: 35g | Fiber: 12g | Sugars: 6g | Total Fat: 6g | Saturated Fat: 1g | Cholesterol: 0mg | Sodium: 600mg | Potassium: 750mg

Micronutrients:

Vitamin A: 100% Daily Value | Vitamin C: 50% Daily Value | Calcium: 15% Daily Value | Iron: 25% Daily Value

24. Turkey and Avocado Club Sandwich on Whole Grain Bread

Prep.Time: 10 minutes
Total Time: 10 minutes

Equipment Needed: Knife

Difficulty: 1/5

Ingredient List for 2 Servings:
- 2 slices whole grain bread
- 2 ounces turkey breast (60 g)
- 1/4 avocado, sliced (about 50 g)
- 1 leaf romaine lettuce
- 2 tomato slices
- 1 tablespoon mayonnaise (15 ml)
- 1 teaspoon Dijon mustard (5 ml)

Step-by-Step Instructions:
1. **Assembling:** Spread mayonnaise and Dijon mustard on the slices of bread.
2. **Layering:** Layer the turkey, avocado, lettuce, and tomato slices between the two pieces of bread.
3. **Serving:** Cut in half and serve immediately.

Macronutrients:

Calories: 500 kcal | Protein: 25g | Carbohydrates: 40g | Fiber: 8g | Sugars: 6g | Total Fat: 25g | Saturated Fat: 4g | Cholesterol: 50mg | Sodium: 700mg | Potassium: 550mg

Micronutrients:

Vitamin A: 25% Daily Value | Vitamin C: 15% Daily Value | Calcium: 10% Daily Value | Iron: 15% Daily Value

25. Mediterranean Veggie Hummus Wrap

 Prep.Time: 10 minutes
Total Time: 10 minutes

 Equipment Needed: Knife

 Difficulty: 2/5

 Ingredient List for 2 Servings:
- 1 whole wheat tortilla (10-inch, 25 cm)
- 3 tablespoons hummus (45 ml, 45 g)
- 1/4 cup sliced cucumber (60 ml, 40 g)
- 1/4 cup diced red bell pepper (60 ml, 40 g)
- 2 tablespoons crumbled feta cheese (30 ml, 15 g)
- 1 tablespoon olive oil (15 ml)
- 1 tablespoon lemon juice (15 ml)

🏆 **Step-by-Step Instructions:**
1. **Assembling:** Spread hummus on the tortilla. Top with cucumber, red bell pepper, and crumbled feta.
2. **Finishing:** Drizzle with olive oil and lemon juice.
3. **Serving:** Roll up the wrap and serve immediately.

🍽 **Macronutrients:**
Calories: 400 kcal | Protein: 12g | Carbohydrates: 45g | Fiber: 8g | Sugars: 5g | Total Fat: 18g | Saturated Fat: 4g | Cholesterol: 15mg | Sodium: 550mg | Potassium: 400mg

🔬 **Micronutrients:**
Vitamin A: 40% Daily Value | Vitamin C: 90% Daily Value | Calcium: 10% Daily Value | Iron: 10% Daily Value

26. Spinach and Strawberry Salad with Walnuts

 Prep.Time: 10 minutes
Total Time: 10 minutes

 Equipment Needed: Mixing bowl

 Difficulty: 1/5

 Ingredient List for 2 Servings:
- 1 cup fresh spinach (240 ml, 30 g)
- 1/2 cup sliced strawberries (120 ml, 75 g)
- 2 tablespoons chopped walnuts (30 ml, 15 g)
- 1 tablespoon balsamic vinegar (15 ml)
- 1 teaspoon olive oil (5 ml)

🏆 **Step-by-Step Instructions:**
1. **Mixing:** In a bowl, combine spinach, strawberries, and walnuts.
2. **Dressing:** Drizzle with balsamic vinegar and olive oil.
3. **Serving:** Toss and serve immediately.

🍽 **Macronutrients:**
Calories: 300 kcal | Protein: 6g | Carbohydrates: 20g | Fiber: 5g | Sugars: 10g | Total Fat: 20g | Saturated Fat: 2g | Cholesterol: 0mg | Sodium: 30mg | Potassium: 450mg

🔬 **Micronutrients:**
Vitamin A: 60% Daily Value | Vitamin C: 140% Daily Value | Calcium: 10% Daily Value | Iron: 10% Daily Value

27. Soba Noodle Salad with Edamame and Ginger Dressing

Prep. Time: 10 minutes
Cook Time: 5 minutes
Total Time: 15 minutes

Equipment Needed: Saucepan, mixing bowl

Difficulty: 2/5

Ingredient List for 1 Serving:

- 1/2 cup soba noodles, cooked (90 g)
- 1/4 cup shelled edamame (60 ml, 40 g)
- 1/4 cup shredded carrots (60 ml, 30 g)
- 1 tablespoon soy sauce (15 ml)
- 1 teaspoon grated ginger (5 g)
- 1 teaspoon sesame oil (5 ml)
- 1 teaspoon rice vinegar (5 ml)

Step-by-Step Instructions:

1. **Cooking Noodles:** Cook soba noodles according to package instructions. Drain and cool.
2. **Mixing:** In a bowl, combine soba noodles, edamame, and shredded carrots.
3. **Dressing:** In a separate bowl, whisk together soy sauce, ginger, sesame oil, and rice vinegar. Pour over the noodle salad.
4. **Serving:** Toss and serve chilled.

Macronutrients:

Calories: 380 kcal | Protein: 15g | Carbohydrates: 50g | Fiber: 6g | Sugars: 3g | Total Fat: 10g | Saturated Fat: 1g | Cholesterol: 0mg | Sodium: 550mg | Potassium: 350mg

Micronutrients:

Vitamin A: 90% Daily Value | Vitamin C: 20% Daily Value | Calcium: 8% Daily Value | Iron: 15% Daily Value

28. Roasted Beet and Goat Cheese Salad

Prep. Time: 10 minutes
Cook Time: 30 minutes
Total Time: 40 minutes

Equipment Needed: Baking sheet, mixing bowl

Difficulty: 2/5

Ingredient List for 1 Serving:

- 2 small beets, peeled and cubed (200 g)
- 2 tablespoons goat cheese, crumbled (30 ml, 15 g)
- 1 cup mixed greens (240 ml, 30 g)
- 1 tablespoon olive oil (15 ml)
- 1 tablespoon balsamic vinegar (15 ml)

Step-by-Step Instructions:

1. **Roasting Beets:** Preheat the oven to 400°F (200°C). Toss the beet cubes with olive oil and roast on a baking sheet for 30 minutes, or until tender.
2. **Assembling Salad:** In a bowl, mix roasted beets with mixed greens and goat cheese.
3. **Dressing:** Drizzle with balsamic vinegar and toss lightly.
4. **Serving:** Serve immediately.

Macronutrients:

Calories: 350 kcal | Protein: 8g | Carbohydrates: 25g | Fiber: 6g | Sugars: 18g | Total Fat: 22g | Saturated Fat: 5g | Cholesterol: 10mg | Sodium: 200mg | Potassium: 600mg

Micronutrients:

Vitamin A: 40% Daily Value | Vitamin C: 15% Daily Value | Calcium: 8% Daily Value | Iron: 10% Daily Value

29. Tuna Salad Stuffed Avocados

- **Prep.Time:** 10 minutes
  Total Time: 10 minutes

- **Equipment Needed:** Mixing bowl, knife

- **Difficulty:** 2/5

- **Ingredient List for 1 Serving:**
  - 1/2 avocado, halved and pitted (about 75 g)
  - 1/4 cup canned tuna in water, drained (60 ml, 40 g)
  - 1 tablespoon Greek yogurt (15 ml, 15 g)
  - 1 teaspoon lemon juice (5 ml)
  - 1 teaspoon Dijon mustard (5 ml)

Step-by-Step Instructions:
1. **Mixing:** In a bowl, mix tuna, Greek yogurt, lemon juice, and Dijon mustard.
2. **Serving:** Scoop the tuna mixture into the avocado halves and serve immediately.

Macronutrients:
Calories: 320 kcal | Protein: 18g | Carbohydrates: 12g | Fiber: 8g | Sugars: 2g | Total Fat: 24g | Saturated Fat: 3g | Cholesterol: 35mg | Sodium: 220mg | Potassium: 600mg

Micronutrients:
Vitamin A: 6% Daily Value | Vitamin C: 20% Daily Value | Calcium: 8% Daily Value | Iron: 10% Daily Value

30. Butternut Squash and Black Bean Chili

- **Prep.Time:** 10 minutes
  Cook Time: 40 minutes
  Total Time: 50 minutes

- **Equipment Needed:** Large pot, spoon

- **Difficulty:** 3/5

- **Ingredient List for 1 Serving:**
  - 1/2 small butternut squash, peeled and diced (about 200 g)
  - 1/2 cup black beans, cooked (120 ml, 80 g)
  - 1 cup diced tomatoes (240 ml, 200 g)
  - 1/4 cup diced onion (60 ml, 40 g)
  - 1 tablespoon chili powder (15 ml)
  - 1 teaspoon cumin (5 g)
  - 1 tablespoon olive oil (15 ml)
  - Salt and pepper to taste

Step-by-Step Instructions:
1. **Sautéing Veggies:** Heat olive oil in a large pot over medium heat. Add onions and squash, and sauté for 5-7 minutes until softened.
2. **Cooking Chili:** Add black beans, diced tomatoes, chili powder, and cumin. Bring to a simmer and cook for 30-35 minutes until the squash is tender.
3. **Serving:** Season with salt and pepper and serve hot.

Macronutrients:
Calories: 270 kcal | Protein: 10g | Carbohydrates: 50g | Fiber: 12g | Sugars: 8g | Total Fat: 6g | Saturated Fat: 1g | Cholesterol: 0mg | Sodium: 350mg | Potassium: 900mg

Micronutrients:
Vitamin A: 200% Daily Value | Vitamin C: 40% Daily Value | Calcium: 15% Daily Value | Iron: 15% Daily Value

31. Farro Salad with Cherry Tomatoes, Cucumbers, and Feta

 Prep.Time: 10 minutes
Cook Time: 25 minutes
Total Time: 35 minutes

 Equipment Needed: Saucepan, mixing bowl

 Difficulty: 2/5

 Ingredient List for 1 Serving:

- 1/2 cup farro (90 g)
- 1 cup water (240 ml)
- 1/2 cup cherry tomatoes, halved (120 ml, 80 g)
- 1/4 cup diced cucumber (60 ml, 40 g)
- 2 tablespoons feta cheese, crumbled (30 ml, 15 g)
- 1 tablespoon olive oil (15 ml)
- 1 tablespoon lemon juice (15 ml)
- Salt and pepper to taste

Step-by-Step Instructions:

1. **Cooking Farro:** Bring farro and water to a boil, then reduce to a simmer. Cook for 20-25 minutes until tender. Drain and cool.
2. **Mixing Salad:** In a bowl, mix farro, cherry tomatoes, cucumber, and feta. Drizzle with olive oil and lemon juice. Season with salt and pepper.
3. **Serving:** Toss and serve chilled or at room temperature.

Macronutrients:

Calories: 350 kcal | Protein: 10g | Carbohydrates: 45g | Fiber: 8g | Sugars: 5g | Total Fat: 12g | Saturated Fat: 3g | Cholesterol: 10mg | Sodium: 200mg | Potassium: 350mg

Micronutrients:

Vitamin A: 10% Daily Value | Vitamin C: 15% Daily Value | Calcium: 8% Daily Value | Iron: 15% Daily Value

32. Turkey, Spinach, and Tomato Wrap

 Prep.Time: 10 minutes
Total Time: 10 minutes

 Equipment Needed: Knife, blender

 Difficulty: 2/5

 Ingredient List for 1 Serving:

- 1 whole wheat tortilla (10-inch, 25 cm)
- 2 ounces turkey breast (60 g)
- 1/4 cup fresh spinach (60 ml, 20 g)
- 2 slices tomato
- 1/4 avocado, mashed (about 50 g)
- 1 tablespoon Greek yogurt (15 ml)
- 1 teaspoon lemon juice (5 ml)

Step-by-Step Instructions:

1. **Making Avocado Sauce:** In a blender, combine avocado, Greek yogurt, and lemon juice. Blend until smooth.
2. **Assembling Wrap:** Spread the avocado sauce on the tortilla, then layer with turkey, spinach, and tomato slices.
3. **Serving:** Roll up the wrap and serve immediately.

Macronutrients:

Calories: 400 kcal | Protein: 20g | Carbohydrates: 40g | Fiber: 8g | Sugars: 5g | Total Fat: 18g | Saturated Fat: 3g | Cholesterol: 40mg | Sodium: 450mg | Potassium: 500mg

Micronutrients:

Vitamin A: 30% Daily Value | Vitamin C: 15% Daily Value | Calcium: 10% Daily Value | Iron: 10% Daily Value

33. Pea Soup with Mint and Yogurt

Prep.Time: 10 minutes
Cook Time: 20 minutes |
Total Time: 30 minutes

Equipment Needed: Blender, saucepan

Difficulty: 2/5

Ingredient List for 1 Serving:
- 1 cup frozen peas (240 ml, 150 g)
- 1/4 cup fresh mint leaves (60 ml, 15 g)
- 1 cup vegetable broth (240 ml)
- 1/4 cup Greek yogurt (60 ml, 60 g)
- 1 tablespoon olive oil (15 ml)
- Salt and pepper to taste

Step-by-Step Instructions:
1. **Cooking Peas:** In a saucepan, bring the vegetable broth to a boil. Add the peas and cook for 5-7 minutes.
2. **Blending:** Blend the cooked peas, mint leaves, and olive oil until smooth. Season with salt and pepper.
3. **Serving:** Pour the soup into bowls and garnish with Greek yogurt. Serve warm.

Macronutrients:
Calories: 180 kcal | Protein: 6g | Carbohydrates: 20g | Fiber: 6g | Sugars: 6g | Total Fat: 9g | Saturated Fat: 2g | Cholesterol: 5mg | Sodium: 500mg | Potassium: 300mg

Micronutrients:
Vitamin A: 20% Daily Value | Vitamin C: 60% Daily Value | Calcium: 8% Daily Value | Iron: 10% Daily Value

34. Brown Rice Salad with Chickpeas, Carrots, and Zucchini

Prep.Time: 10 minutes
Cook Time: 20 minutes
Total Time: 30 minutes

Equipment Needed: Saucepan, mixing bowl

Difficulty: 2/5

Ingredient List for 1 Serving:
- 1/2 cup brown rice (90 g)
- 1/4 cup cooked chickpeas (60 ml, 40 g)
- 1/4 cup diced carrots (60 ml, 30 g)
- 1/4 cup diced zucchini (60 ml, 30 g)
- 1 tablespoon olive oil (15 ml)
- 1 tablespoon lemon juice (15 ml)
- Salt and pepper to taste

Step-by-Step Instructions:
1. **Cooking Rice:** Cook the brown rice in water according to package instructions, about 20 minutes. Let cool.
2. **Assembling Salad:** In a bowl, combine the cooked rice, chickpeas, carrots, and zucchini. Drizzle with olive oil and lemon juice.
3. **Serving:** Serve at room temperature or chilled.

Macronutrients:
Calories: 380 kcal | Protein: 9g | Carbohydrates: 60g | Fiber: 8g | Sugars: 5g | Total Fat: 12g | Saturated Fat: 1.5g | Cholesterol: 0mg | Sodium: 200mg | Potassium: 450mg

Micronutrients:
Vitamin A: 50% Daily Value | Vitamin C: 20% Daily Value | Calcium: 6% Daily Value | Iron: 15% Daily Value

35. Grilled Chicken with Couscous Salad and Roasted Veggies

Prep.Time: 15 minutes
Cook Time: 20 minutes
Total Time: 35 minutes

Equipment Needed: Grill or skillet, saucepan, baking sheet

Difficulty: 3/5

Ingredient List for 1 Serving:
- 2 small chicken breasts (4 oz each, 120 g)
- 1/2 cup couscous (90 g)
- 1/4 cup diced bell peppers (60 ml, 30 g)
- 1/4 cup zucchini, sliced (60 ml, 30 g)
- 1 tablespoon olive oil (15 ml)
- 1 tablespoon lemon juice (15 ml)
- Salt and pepper to taste

🏆 Step-by-Step Instructions:

1. **Grilling Chicken:** Season the chicken with salt and pepper. Grill or cook in a skillet over medium heat for 5-7 minutes per side.
2. **Cooking Couscous:** Prepare couscous according to package instructions. Let cool slightly.
3. **Roasting Veggies:** Preheat oven to 400°F (200°C). Toss the bell peppers and zucchini with olive oil, then roast on a baking sheet for 15-20 minutes until tender.
4. **Serving:** Serve the grilled chicken with couscous salad, topped with roasted veggies and drizzled with lemon juice.

🍽 Macronutrients:
Calories: 450 kcal | Protein: 30g | Carbohydrates: 45g | Fiber: 6g | Sugars: 7g | Total Fat: 15g | Saturated Fat: 3g | Cholesterol: 70mg | Sodium: 250mg | Potassium: 550mg

🔬 Micronutrients:
Vitamin A: 15% Daily Value | Vitamin C: 50% Daily Value | Calcium: 4% Daily Value | Iron: 10% Daily Value

36. Kale Salad with Almonds and Oranges

Prep.Time: 10 minutes
Total Time: 10 minutes

Equipment Needed: Mixing bowl

Difficulty: 1/5

Ingredient List for 1 Serving:
- 2 cups kale, chopped (480 ml, 60 g)
- 1 small orange, segmented (about 100 g)
- 2 tablespoons sliced almonds (30 ml, 15 g)
- 1 tablespoon olive oil (15 ml)
- 1 tablespoon lemon juice (15 ml)
- Salt and pepper to taste

🏆 Step-by-Step Instructions:

1. **Massaging Kale:** In a bowl, toss the chopped kale with olive oil and lemon juice. Massage for 1-2 minutes until the kale softens.
2. **Assembling Salad:** Add the orange segments and sliced almonds. Toss to combine.
3. **Serving:** Serve immediately as a refreshing salad.

🍽 Macronutrients:
Calories: 280 kcal | Protein: 5g | Carbohydrates: 25g | Fiber: 7g | Sugars: 10g | Total Fat: 18g | Saturated Fat: 2g | Cholesterol: 0mg | Sodium: 150mg | Potassium: 500mg

🔬 Micronutrients:
Vitamin A: 200% Daily Value | Vitamin C: 150% Daily Value | Calcium: 15% Daily Value | Iron: 10% Daily Value

37. Smoked Salmon and Avocado Sandwich on Rye Bread

 Prep. Time: 5 minutes
Total Time: 5 minutes

 Equipment Needed: Knife

 Difficulty: 1/5

 Ingredient List for 1 Serving:
- 2 slices rye bread (about 60 g)
- 2 oz smoked salmon (60 g)
- 1/4 avocado, mashed (about 50 g)
- 1 tablespoon lemon juice (15 ml)
- Fresh dill for garnish (optional)

🏆 Step-by-Step Instructions:
1. **Preparing Avocado:** In a bowl, mash the avocado with lemon juice.
2. **Assembling Sandwich:** Spread the avocado mixture on the rye bread slices. Top with smoked salmon and garnish with fresh dill.
3. **Serving:** Serve immediately.

🍽 Macronutrients:
Calories: 370 kcal | Protein: 14g | Carbohydrates: 30g | Fiber: 8g | Sugars: 2g | Total Fat: 20g | Saturated Fat: 3g | Cholesterol: 30mg | Sodium: 800mg | Potassium: 550mg

🔬 Micronutrients:
Vitamin A: 10% Daily Value | Vitamin C: 15% Daily Value | Calcium: 4% Daily Value | Iron: 15% Daily Value

38. Chickpea Salad with Sundried Tomatoes and Arugula

 Prep. Time: 10 minutes
Total Time: 10 minutes

 Equipment Needed: Mixing bowl

 Difficulty: 1/5

 Ingredient List for 1 Serving:
- 1/2 cup cooked chickpeas (120 ml, 80 g)
- 1/4 cup sundried tomatoes, chopped (60 ml, 20 g)
- 1/2 cup fresh arugula (120 ml, 20 g)
- 1 tablespoon olive oil (15 ml)
- 1 tablespoon balsamic vinegar (15 ml)
- Salt and pepper to taste

🏆 Step-by-Step Instructions:
1. **Assembling Salad:** In a bowl, combine chickpeas, sundried tomatoes, and arugula.
2. **Dressing:** Drizzle with olive oil and balsamic vinegar. Toss to coat.
3. **Serving:** Serve immediately as a hearty salad.

🍽 Macronutrients:
Calories: 300 kcal | Protein: 8g | Carbohydrates: 30g | Fiber: 8g | Sugars: 6g | Total Fat: 16g | Saturated Fat: 2g | Cholesterol: 0mg | Sodium: 350mg | Potassium: 450mg

🔬 Micronutrients:
Vitamin A: 8% Daily Value | Vitamin C: 10% Daily Value | Calcium: 6% Daily Value | Iron: 15% Daily Value

39. Hummus and Grilled Vegetable Wrap with Tahini Sauce

 Prep.Time: 10 minutes
Cook Time: 10 minutes
Total Time: 20 minutes

 Equipment Needed: Skillet, mixing bowl

 Difficulty: 2/5

 Ingredient List for 2 Servings:

- 1 whole wheat tortilla
- 2 tablespoons hummus (30 ml, 30 g)
- 1/4 cup sliced zucchini (60 ml, 30 g)
- 1/4 cup sliced bell peppers (60 ml, 30 g)
- 1 tablespoon tahini (15 ml)
- 1 tablespoon lemon juice (15 ml)

🏆 Step-by-Step Instructions:

1. **Grilling Vegetables:** In a skillet, grill zucchini and bell peppers for 5-7 minutes until tender.
2. **Assembling Wrap:** Spread the hummus on the tortilla. Add the grilled vegetables.
3. **Tahini Sauce:** Mix tahini and lemon juice in a bowl. Drizzle over the wrap filling.
4. **Serving:** Roll up the tortilla and serve warm.

🍽 Macronutrients:

Calories: 350 kcal | Protein: 10g | Carbohydrates: 45g | Fiber: 10g | Sugars: 6g | Total Fat: 15g | Saturated Fat: 2g | Cholesterol: 0mg | Sodium: 350mg | Potassium: 500mg

🔬 Micronutrients:

Vitamin A: 20% Daily Value | Vitamin C: 60% Daily Value | Calcium: 10% Daily Value | Iron: 15% Daily Value

40. Broccoli and Spinach Soup with Sunflower Seeds

 Prep.Time: 10 minutes
Cook Time: 15 minutes
Total Time: 25 minutes

 Equipment Needed: Blender, saucepan

 Difficulty: 2/5

 Ingredient List for 1 Serving:

- 1 cup broccoli florets (240 ml, 60 g)
- 1/2 cup fresh spinach (120 ml, 30 g)
- 1 tablespoon sunflower seeds (15 ml)
- 2 cups vegetable broth (480 ml)
- 1 tablespoon olive oil (15 ml)
- Salt and pepper to taste

🏆 Step-by-Step Instructions:

1. **Cooking Vegetables:** In a saucepan, bring vegetable broth to a boil. Add broccoli and cook for 10 minutes. Add spinach and cook for 2 more minutes.
2. **Blending:** Blend the soup until smooth.
3. **Serving:** Garnish with sunflower seeds and serve warm.

🍽 Macronutrients:

Calories: 200 kcal | Protein: 6g | Carbohydrates: 18g | Fiber: 5g | Sugars: 5g | Total Fat: 12g | Saturated Fat: 2g | Cholesterol: 0mg | Sodium: 400mg | Potassium: 450mg

🔬 Micronutrients:

Vitamin A: 60% Daily Value | Vitamin C: 100% Daily Value | Calcium: 8% Daily Value | Iron: 10% Daily Value

3.3 DINNER

41. Grilled Salmon with Quinoa and Broccoli

Prep.Time: 10 minutes
Cook Time: 20 minutes
Total Time: 30 minutes

Equipment Needed: Grill or skillet, saucepan

Difficulty: 3/5

Ingredient List for 1 Serving:
- 2 salmon fillets (4 oz each, 120 g)
- 1/2 cup quinoa, rinsed (90 g)
- 1 cup broccoli florets (240 ml, 60 g)
- 1 tablespoon olive oil (15 ml)
- Salt and pepper to taste

Step-by-Step Instructions:
1. **Grilling Salmon:** Season salmon with salt and pepper. Grill or cook in a skillet over medium heat for 5-7 minutes per side.
2. **Cooking Quinoa:** In a saucepan, cook quinoa in 1 cup of water (240 ml) until absorbed, about 15 minutes.
3. **Steaming Broccoli:** Steam the broccoli until tender, about 5 minutes.
4. **Serving:** Serve grilled salmon with quinoa and broccoli on the side, drizzled with olive oil.

Macronutrients:
Calories: 500 kcal | Protein: 35g | Carbohydrates: 40g | Fiber: 8g | Sugars: 2g | Total Fat: 20g | Saturated Fat: 3g | Cholesterol: 70mg | Sodium: 180mg | Potassium: 750mg

Micronutrients:
Vitamin A: 15% Daily Value | Vitamin C: 100% Daily Value | Calcium: 6% Daily Value | Iron: 20% Daily Value

42. Baked Chicken with Sweet Potatoes

Prep.Time: 10 minutes
Cook Time: 35 minutes
Total Time: 45 minutes

Equipment Needed: Baking sheet, oven

Difficulty: 2/5

Ingredient List for 1 Serving:
- 2 small chicken breasts (4 oz each, 120 g)
- 1 medium sweet potato, diced (about 150 g)
- 1/2 cup Brussels sprouts, halved (120 ml, 60 g)
- 1 tablespoon olive oil (15 ml)
- 1 teaspoon paprika (5 ml)
- Salt and pepper to taste

Step-by-Step Instructions:
1. **Prepping Chicken and Vegetables:** Preheat the oven to 375°F (190°C). Toss the diced sweet potatoes and Brussels sprouts with olive oil, paprika, salt, and pepper. Arrange on a baking sheet with the chicken breasts.
2. **Baking:** Bake for 35 minutes or until the chicken is fully cooked and the vegetables are tender.
3. **Serving:** Serve the baked chicken with sweet potatoes and Brussels sprouts.

Macronutrients:
Calories: 450 kcal | Protein: 30g | Carbohydrates: 35g | Fiber: 7g | Sugars: 8g | Total Fat: 20g | Saturated Fat: 3g | Cholesterol: 70mg | Sodium: 180mg | Potassium: 750mg

Micronutrients:
Vitamin A: 200% Daily Value | Vitamin C: 60% Daily Value | Calcium: 6% Daily Value | Iron: 10% Daily Value

47. Cauliflower Steak with Herb Quinoa Salad

 Prep.Time: 10 minutes
Cook Time: 20 minutes
Total Time: 30 minutes

 Equipment Needed: Baking sheet, saucepan

 Difficulty: 2/5

 Ingredient List for 1 Serving:
- 2 cauliflower "steaks" (cut from a medium cauliflower, about 200 g total)
- 1/2 cup quinoa (120 ml, 90 g)
- 1 tablespoon olive oil (15 ml)
- 1 tablespoon fresh parsley, chopped (15 ml)
- 1 tablespoon lemon juice (15 ml)
- Salt and pepper to taste

Step-by-Step Instructions:
1. **Roasting Cauliflower:** Preheat the oven to 400°F (200°C). Brush cauliflower steaks with olive oil and roast on a baking sheet for 20 minutes until tender and golden.
2. **Cooking Quinoa:** In a saucepan, cook quinoa in water according to package instructions, about 15 minutes. Let cool slightly.
3. **Mixing Salad:** In a bowl, mix cooked quinoa with parsley, lemon juice, salt, and pepper.
4. **Serving:** Serve cauliflower steaks with quinoa salad on the side.

Macronutrients:
Calories: 350 kcal | Protein: 12g | Carbohydrates: 50g | Fiber: 10g | Sugars: 7g | Total Fat: 12g | Saturated Fat: 1.5g | Cholesterol: 0mg | Sodium: 180mg | Potassium: 1000mg

Micronutrients:
Vitamin A: 20% Daily Value | Vitamin C: 200% Daily Value | Calcium: 8% Daily Value | Iron: 15% Daily Value

48. Baked Cod with Ratatouille

 Prep.Time: 15 minutes
Cook Time: 30 minutes
Total Time: 45 minutes

 Equipment Needed: Baking sheet, skillet

 Difficulty: 3/5

 Ingredient List for 1 Serving:
- 2 cod fillets (4 oz each, 120 g)
- 1/2 cup diced eggplant (120 ml, 60 g)
- 1/2 cup diced zucchini (120 ml, 60 g)
- 1/4 cup diced bell peppers (60 ml, 30 g)
- 1/4 cup diced tomatoes (60 ml, 40 g)
- 1 tablespoon olive oil (15 ml)
- 1 teaspoon fresh thyme (5 ml)
- Salt and pepper to taste

Step-by-Step Instructions:
1. **Cooking Ratatouille:** In a skillet, heat olive oil over medium heat. Add eggplant, zucchini, bell peppers, and tomatoes. Sauté for 10-12 minutes until tender. Stir in thyme and season with salt and pepper.
2. **Baking Cod:** Preheat oven to 375°F (190°C). Season cod fillets with salt and pepper, and bake on a baking sheet for 12-15 minutes, or until the fish is cooked through and flakes easily.
3. **Serving:** Serve baked cod on a bed of ratatouille.

Macronutrients:
Calories: 400 kcal | Protein: 35g | Carbohydrates: 25g | Fiber: 8g | Sugars: 10g | Total Fat: 15g | Saturated Fat: 2g | Cholesterol: 70mg | Sodium: 180mg | Potassium: 1000mg

Micronutrients:
Vitamin A: 30% Daily Value | Vitamin C: 80% Daily Value | Calcium: 6% Daily Value | Iron: 15% Daily Value

49. Turkey Meatballs in Tomato Basil Sauce

- **Prep. Time:** 15 minutes
  Cook Time: 25 minutes
  Total Time: 40 minutes
- **Equipment Needed:** Mixing bowl, baking sheet, saucepan
- **Difficulty:** 2/5
- **Ingredient List for 1 Serving:**
  - 1/2 pound ground turkey (225 g)
  - 1/4 cup breadcrumbs (60 ml, 30 g)
  - 1 large egg
  - 1/4 cup grated Parmesan cheese (60 ml, 30 g)
  - 1 tablespoon olive oil (15 ml)
  - 1 cup tomato sauce (240 ml)
  - 1/4 cup fresh basil, chopped (60 ml)
  - Salt and pepper to taste

Step-by-Step Instructions:

1. **Mixing Meatballs:** Preheat oven to 375°F (190°C). In a mixing bowl, combine ground turkey, breadcrumbs, egg, Parmesan, salt, and pepper. Form into small meatballs.
2. **Baking Meatballs:** Place meatballs on a baking sheet and bake for 15-20 minutes until browned and cooked through.
3. **Cooking Sauce:** In a saucepan, heat olive oil over medium heat. Add tomato sauce and fresh basil. Simmer for 5 minutes.
4. **Serving:** Add the baked meatballs to the sauce and serve hot.

Macronutrients:

Calories: 330 kcal | Protein: 28g | Carbohydrates: 15g | Fiber: 2g | Sugars: 6g | Total Fat: 18g | Saturated Fat: 5g | Cholesterol: 130mg | Sodium: 450mg | Potassium: 600mg

Micronutrients:

Vitamin A: 10% Daily Value | Vitamin C: 20% Daily Value | Calcium: 15% Daily Value | Iron: 15% Daily Value

50. Caprese Salad with Balsamic Reduction

- **Prep. Time:** 10 minutes
  Cook Time: 40 minutes
  Total Time: 50 minutes
- **Equipment Needed:** Baking sheet, skillet
- **Difficulty:** 2/5
- **Ingredient List for 1 Serving:**
  - 1 medium spaghetti squash (about 600 g)
  - 1 cup fresh spinach (240 ml, 30 g)
  - 1/4 cup crumbled feta cheese (60 ml, 30 g)
  - 1 tablespoon olive oil (15 ml)
  - 1/4 teaspoon garlic powder (1.25 g)
  - Salt and pepper to taste

Step-by-Step Instructions:

1. **Baking Squash:** Preheat oven to 375°F (190°C). Cut the spaghetti squash in half and remove seeds. Brush with olive oil and bake for 35-40 minutes until tender. Scrape the flesh with a fork to create "spaghetti" strands.
2. **Cooking Spinach:** In a skillet, heat olive oil over medium heat. Add spinach and sauté for 2-3 minutes until wilted. Stir in garlic powder.
3. **Assembling:** Mix the spaghetti squash with sautéed spinach and crumbled feta. Season with salt and pepper. Serve warm.

Macronutrients:

Calories: 310 kcal | Protein: 9g | Carbohydrates: 35g | Fiber: 8g | Sugars: 9g | Total Fat: 15g | Saturated Fat: 5g | Cholesterol: 20mg | Sodium: 400mg | Potassium: 850mg

Micronutrients:

Vitamin A: 50% Daily Value | Vitamin C: 30% Daily Value | Calcium: 15% Daily Value | Iron: 10% Daily Value

51. Red Lentil and Spinach Soup

Prep. Time: 10 minutes
Cook Time: 20 minutes
Total Time: 30 minutes

Equipment Needed: Large pot, spoon

Difficulty: 2/5

Ingredient List for 1 Serving:
- 1/2 cup red lentils (90 g)
- 1/2 cup fresh spinach (120 ml, 30 g)
- 1 small carrot, diced (about 60 g)
- 1/4 cup diced onions (60 ml, 40 g)
- 2 cups vegetable broth (480 ml)
- 1 tablespoon olive oil (15 ml)
- 1/2 teaspoon cumin (2.5 g)
- Salt and pepper to taste

Step-by-Step Instructions:
1. **Sautéing Vegetables:** Heat olive oil in a large pot over medium heat. Add onions and carrots, and sauté for 5-7 minutes until softened.
2. **Cooking Soup:** Add lentils, broth, cumin, salt, and pepper. Bring to a boil, then reduce heat and simmer for 15-20 minutes until lentils are tender.
3. **Finishing:** Stir in fresh spinach during the last 5 minutes of cooking.
4. **Serving:** Serve hot with a drizzle of olive oil on top.

Macronutrients:
Calories: 300 kcal | Protein: 16g | Carbohydrates: 40g | Fiber: 15g | Sugars: 6g | Total Fat: 10g | Saturated Fat: 1.5g | Cholesterol: 0mg | Sodium: 450mg | Potassium: 750mg

Micronutrients:
Vitamin A: 90% Daily Value | Vitamin C: 40% Daily Value | Calcium: 10% Daily Value | Iron: 25% Daily Value

52. Baked Salmon with Herbs and Roasted Sweet Potatoes

Prep. Time: 10 minutes
Cook Time: 30 minutes
Total Time: 40 minutes

Equipment Needed: Baking sheet

Difficulty: 2/5

Ingredient List for 1 Serving:
- salmon fillets (4 oz each, 120 g)
- 1 medium sweet potato, diced (about 150 g)
- 1 tablespoon olive oil (15 ml)
- 1 teaspoon fresh rosemary, chopped (5 ml)
- 1 teaspoon lemon juice (5 ml)
- Salt and pepper to taste

Step-by-Step Instructions:
1. **Roasting Sweet Potatoes:** Preheat the oven to 400°F (200°C). Toss diced sweet potatoes with half of the olive oil, rosemary, salt, and pepper. Spread on a baking sheet and roast for 25-30 minutes, flipping halfway through.
2. **Baking Salmon:** Season salmon fillets with salt, pepper, and lemon juice. Place on a baking sheet and bake for 12-15 minutes until fully cooked.
3. **Serving:** Serve the salmon alongside roasted sweet potatoes.

Macronutrients:
Calories: 450 kcal | Protein: 30g | Carbohydrates: 30g | Fiber: 5g | Sugars: 8g | Total Fat: 24g | Saturated Fat: 4g | Cholesterol: 65mg | Sodium: 150mg | Potassium: 800mg

Micronutrients:
Vitamin A: 200% Daily Value | Vitamin C: 20% Daily Value | Calcium: 6% Daily Value | Iron: 10% Daily Value

53. Grilled Chicken with Avocado Sauce and Quinoa Salad

Prep.Time: 10 minutes
Cook Time: 20 minutes
Total Time: 30 minutes
Equipment Needed: Grill or skillet, saucepan, blender

Difficulty: 3/5

Ingredient List for 1 Serving:
- 2 small chicken breasts (4 oz each, 120 g)
- 1/2 cup quinoa, rinsed (90 g)
- 1 cup water (240 ml)
- 1/4 avocado (about 50 g)
- 1 tablespoon lemon juice (15 ml)
- 1 tablespoon olive oil (15 ml)
- Salt and pepper to taste

Step-by-Step Instructions:
1. **Grilling Chicken:** Season chicken with salt and pepper. Grill or cook in a skillet for 5-7 minutes per side until fully cooked.
2. **Cooking Quinoa:** In a saucepan, bring water to a boil. Add quinoa, cover, and simmer for 15 minutes until water is absorbed. Let cool.
3. **Making Avocado Sauce:** In a blender, blend avocado, lemon juice, olive oil, salt, and pepper until smooth.
4. **Serving:** Serve grilled chicken over quinoa, drizzled with avocado sauce.

Macronutrients:
Calories: 420 kcal | Protein: 30g | Carbohydrates: 35g | Fiber: 7g | Sugars: 2g | Total Fat: 18g | Saturated Fat: 3g | Cholesterol: 65mg | Sodium: 150mg | Potassium: 700mg

Micronutrients:
Vitamin A: 6% Daily Value | Vitamin C: 15% Daily Value | Calcium: 4% Daily Value | Iron: 15% Daily Value

54. Grilled Tofu with Miso Sauce and Stir-Fried Vegetables

Prep.Time: 10 minutes
Cook Time: 20 minutes
Total Time: 30 minutes
Equipment Needed: Grill or skillet, mixing bowl, wok

Difficulty: 3/5

Ingredient List for 1 Serving:
- 1/2 block tofu, cubed (120 g)
- 1 tablespoon miso paste (15 ml)
- 1 tablespoon soy sauce (15 ml)
- 1 tablespoon sesame oil (15 ml)
- 1/4 cup sliced bell peppers (60 ml, 30 g)
- 1/4 cup sliced carrots (60 ml, 30 g)
- 1/4 cup broccoli florets (60 ml, 30 g)

Step-by-Step Instructions:
1. **Grilling Tofu:** Mix miso paste, soy sauce, and sesame oil. Marinate tofu cubes in the mixture for 10 minutes. Grill tofu for 3-4 minutes per side until golden brown.
2. **Stir-Frying Vegetables:** In a wok, stir-fry bell peppers, carrots, and broccoli in sesame oil over medium heat for 5-7 minutes until tender.
3. **Serving:** Serve grilled tofu over stir-fried vegetables, drizzled with any remaining miso sauce.

Macronutrients:
Calories: 380 kcal | Protein: 16g | Carbohydrates: 22g | Fiber: 6g | Sugars: 6g | Total Fat: 24g | Saturated Fat: 3g | Cholesterol: 0mg | Sodium: 700mg | Potassium: 500mg

Micronutrients:
Vitamin A: 100% Daily Value | Vitamin C: 80% Daily Value | Calcium: 10% Daily Value | Iron: 20% Daily Value

55. Brown Rice Risotto with Mushrooms and Parmesan

Prep. Time: 10 minutes
Cook Time: 10 minutes
Total Time: 20 minutes

Equipment Needed: Large saucepan

Difficulty: 3/5

Ingredient List for 1 Serving:
- 1/2 cup brown rice (90 g)
- 1 1/2 cups vegetable broth (360 ml)
- 1/2 cup sliced mushrooms (120 ml, 60 g)
- 1/4 cup grated Parmesan cheese (60 ml, 30 g)
- 1 tablespoon olive oil (15 ml)
- 1/4 cup diced onions (60 ml, 40 g)
- Salt and pepper to taste

Step-by-Step Instructions:
1. **Sautéing Vegetables:** In a large saucepan, heat olive oil over medium heat. Sauté onions and mushrooms for 5-7 minutes until softened.
2. **Cooking Rice:** Add brown rice to the saucepan and stir for 1-2 minutes. Gradually add vegetable broth, 1/2 cup at a time, allowing the rice to absorb the liquid before adding more. Cook for 25-30 minutes until the rice is tender.
3. **Finishing:** Stir in Parmesan cheese, salt, and pepper.
4. **Serving:** Serve warm.

Macronutrients:
Calories: 400 kcal | Protein: 12g | Carbohydrates: 55g | Fiber: 5g | Sugars: 4g | Total Fat: 12g | Saturated Fat: 3g | Cholesterol: 10mg | Sodium: 450mg | Potassium: 500mg

Micronutrients:
Vitamin A: 4% Daily Value | Vitamin C: 6% Daily Value | Calcium: 15% Daily Value | Iron: 8% Daily Value

56. Baked Eggplant Parmesan

Prep. Time: 10 minutes
Cook Time: 25 minutes
Total Time: 35 minutes

Equipment Needed: Baking dish, oven

Difficulty: 3/5

Ingredient List for 1 Serving:
- 1 medium eggplant, sliced (about 300 g)
- 1/2 cup marinara sauce (120 ml)
- 1/4 cup shredded mozzarella cheese (60 ml, 30 g)
- 1/4 cup grated Parmesan cheese (60 ml, 30 g)
- 1 tablespoon olive oil (15 ml)
- Salt and pepper to taste

Step-by-Step Instructions:
1. **Prepping Eggplant:** Preheat oven to 375°F (190°C). Brush eggplant slices with olive oil, season with salt and pepper, and bake for 20 minutes until tender.
2. **Assembling:** In a baking dish, layer the baked eggplant slices with marinara sauce, mozzarella, and Parmesan.
3. **Baking:** Return to the oven and bake for 5-7 minutes until the cheese is melted and bubbly.
4. **Serving:** Serve warm.

Macronutrients:
Calories: 350 kcal | Protein: 15g | Carbohydrates: 25g | Fiber: 8g | Sugars: 10g | Total Fat: 20g | Saturated Fat: 7g | Cholesterol: 30mg | Sodium: 550mg | Potassium: 600mg

Micronutrients:
Vitamin A: 10% Daily Value | Vitamin C: 10% Daily Value | Calcium: 25% Daily Value | Iron: 6% Daily Value

57. Sesame-Crusted Salmon with Sautéed Spinach

Prep. Time: 10 minutes
Cook Time: 15 minutes
Total Time: 25 minutes

Equipment Needed: Skillet, mixing bowl

Difficulty: 3/5

Ingredient List for 1 Serving:

- 2 salmon fillets (4 oz each, 120 g)
- 1 tablespoon sesame seeds (15 g)
- 1 tablespoon soy sauce (15 ml)
- 1 tablespoon olive oil (15 ml)
- 1 cup fresh spinach (240 ml, 30 g)
- 1 teaspoon lemon juice (5 ml)

Step-by-Step Instructions:

1. **Preparing Salmon:** Coat each salmon fillet with sesame seeds and soy sauce.
2. **Cooking Salmon:** Heat olive oil in a skillet over medium heat. Cook the salmon for 4-5 minutes per side until fully cooked and crispy.
3. **Sautéing Spinach:** In the same skillet, add spinach and sauté for 2-3 minutes until wilted. Drizzle with lemon juice.
4. **Serving:** Serve sesame-crusted salmon with sautéed spinach on the side.

Macronutrients:

Calories: 400 kcal | Protein: 30g | Carbohydrates: 5g | Fiber: 2g | Sugars: 1g | Total Fat: 28g | Saturated Fat: 4g | Cholesterol: 65mg | Sodium: 400mg | Potassium: 700mg

Micronutrients:

Vitamin A: 50% Daily Value | Vitamin C: 15% Daily Value | Calcium: 10% Daily Value | Iron: 10% Daily Value

58. Chicken Salad with Barley and Crunchy Vegetables

Prep. Time: 10 minutes
Cook Time: 30 minutes
Total Time: 40 minutes

Equipment Needed: Saucepan, mixing bowl

Difficulty: 3/5

Ingredient List for 1 Serving:

- 1/2 cup cooked barley (90 g)
- 1 small chicken breast (4 oz, 120 g), cooked and diced
- 1/4 cup diced cucumbers (60 ml, 30 g)
- 1/4 cup diced red bell pepper (60 ml, 30 g)
- 1 tablespoon olive oil (15 ml)
- 1 tablespoon lemon juice (15 ml)
- Salt and pepper to taste

Step-by-Step Instructions:

1. **Cooking Barley:** Cook barley in water according to package instructions, usually about 30 minutes. Let cool.
2. **Assembling Salad:** In a mixing bowl, combine cooked barley, chicken, cucumbers, and bell peppers. Drizzle with olive oil and lemon juice.
3. **Serving:** Toss and serve chilled or at room temperature.

Macronutrients:

Calories: 370 kcal | Protein: 25g | Carbohydrates: 40g | Fiber: 6g | Sugars: 4g | Total Fat: 12g | Saturated Fat: 2g | Cholesterol: 50mg | Sodium: 200mg | Potassium: 500mg

Micronutrients:

Vitamin A: 20% Daily Value | Vitamin C: 60% Daily Value | Calcium: 4% Daily Value | Iron: 10% Daily Value

59. Farro Pasta with Broccoli and Basil Pesto

Prep. Time: 10 minutes
Cook Time: 15 minutes
Total Time: 25 minutes

Equipment Needed: Saucepan, food processor

Difficulty: 2/5

Ingredient List for 1 Serving:

- 1 cup farro pasta (120 g)
- 1/2 cup broccoli florets (120 ml, 60 g)
- 1/4 cup fresh basil leaves (60 ml, 15 g)
- 1/4 cup grated Parmesan cheese (60 ml, 30 g)
- 1 tablespoon olive oil (15 ml)
- 1 garlic clove, minced

Step-by-Step Instructions:

1. **Cooking Pasta:** Cook farro pasta according to package instructions. Add broccoli to the boiling water during the last 5 minutes of cooking. Drain.
2. **Making Pesto:** In a food processor, blend basil, Parmesan cheese, olive oil, and garlic until smooth.
3. **Assembling:** Toss cooked pasta and broccoli with the pesto sauce. Serve warm.

Macronutrients:

Calories: 390 kcal | Protein: 14g | Carbohydrates: 60g | Fiber: 9g | Sugars: 4g | Total Fat: 10g | Saturated Fat: 3g | Cholesterol: 10mg | Sodium: 200mg | Potassium: 500mg

Micronutrients:

Vitamin A: 20% Daily Value | Vitamin C: 80% Daily Value | Calcium: 20% Daily Value | Iron: 15% Daily Value

60. Pumpkin and Carrot Soup

Prep. Time: 10 minutes
Cook Time: 20 minutes
Total Time: 30 minutes

Equipment Needed: Blender, saucepan

Difficulty: 2/5

Ingredient List for 1 Serving:

- 1 cup diced pumpkin (240 ml, 200 g)
- 1 small carrot, diced (about 60 g)
- 2 cups vegetable broth (480 ml)
- 2 tablespoons Greek yogurt (30 ml, 30 g)
- 1 tablespoon pumpkin seeds (15 ml, 10 g)
- 1 tablespoon olive oil (15 ml)
- Salt and pepper to taste

Step-by-Step Instructions:

1. **Cooking Soup:** In a saucepan, heat olive oil over medium heat. Add pumpkin and carrot, and sauté for 5-7 minutes. Add broth and simmer for 15 minutes until vegetables are tender.
2. **Blending:** Blend the soup until smooth.
3. **Serving:** Serve hot, topped with Greek yogurt and pumpkin seeds.

Macronutrients:

Calories: 250 kcal | Protein: 6g | Carbohydrates: 25g | Fiber: 6g | Sugars: 8g | Total Fat: 12g | Saturated Fat: 2g | Cholesterol: 5mg | Sodium: 450mg | Potassium: 700mg

Micronutrients:

Vitamin A: 300% Daily Value | Vitamin C: 20% Daily Value | Calcium: 10% Daily Value | Iron: 15% Daily Value

3.4 SNACKS

61. Apple Slices with Almond Butter

⏰ Prep.Time: 5 minutes
Total Time: 5 minutes

🛠 **Equipment Needed:** Knife

💪 **Difficulty:** 1/5

🛒 **Ingredient List for 2 Servings:**
- 1 medium apple, sliced (about 180 g)
- 1 tablespoon almond butter (15 ml, 16 g)

🍴 **Step-by-Step Instructions:**
1. **Preparation:** Slice the apple and serve with almond butter for dipping.
2. **Serving:** Serve immediately as a quick snack.

🍽 **Macronutrients:**
Calories: 200 kcal | Protein: 3g | Carbohydrates: 30g | Fiber: 6g | Sugars: 20g | Total Fat: 9g | Saturated Fat: 1g | Cholesterol: 0mg | Sodium: 0mg | Potassium: 220mg

🔬 **Micronutrients:**
Vitamin A: 2% Daily Value | Vitamin C: 10% Daily Value | Calcium: 4% Daily Value | Iron: 2% Daily Value

62. Carrot Sticks with Hummus

⏰ Prep.Time: 5 minutes
Total Time: 5 minutes

🛠 **Equipment Needed:** Knife

💪 **Difficulty:** 1/5

🛒 **Ingredient List for 1 Serving:**
- 1 medium carrot, cut into sticks (about 60 g)
- 2 tablespoons hummus (30 ml, 30 g)

🍴 **Step-by-Step Instructions:**
1. **Preparation:** Slice the carrot into sticks and serve with hummus for dipping.
2. **Serving:** Serve immediately as a healthy snack.

🍽 **Macronutrients:**
Calories: 150 kcal | Protein: 3g | Carbohydrates: 12g | Fiber: 4g | Sugars: 5g | Total Fat: 9g | Saturated Fat: 1g | Cholesterol: 0mg | Sodium: 180mg | Potassium: 250mg

🔬 **Micronutrients:**
Vitamin A: 300% Daily Value | Vitamin C: 6% Daily Value | Calcium: 4% Daily Value | Iron: 4% Daily Value

63. Mixed Nuts and Dried Fruit Trail Mix

Prep. Time: 5 minutes
Total Time: 5 minutes

Equipment Needed: Bowl

Difficulty: 1/5

Ingredient List for 1 Serving:
- 1/4 cup mixed nuts (60 ml, 30 g)
- 1/4 cup dried fruit (60 ml, 30 g)

Step-by-Step Instructions:
1. **Mixing:** Combine mixed nuts and dried fruit in a bowl.
2. **Serving:** Enjoy as a quick snack.

Macronutrients:
Calories: 180 kcal | Protein: 4g | Carbohydrates: 22g | Fiber: 4g | Sugars: 14g | Total Fat: 9g | Saturated Fat: 1g | Cholesterol: 0mg | Sodium: 5mg | Potassium: 300mg

Micronutrients:
Vitamin A: 2% Daily Value | Vitamin C: 0% Daily Value | Calcium: 4% Daily Value | Iron: 6% Daily Value

64. Greek Yogurt with Honey and Cinnamon

Prep. Time: 2 minutes
Total Time: 2 minutes

Equipment Needed: Spoon

Difficulty: 1/5

Ingredient List for 1 Serving:
- 1/2 cup Greek yogurt (120 ml, 125 g)
- 1 teaspoon honey (5 ml)
- 1/4 teaspoon ground cinnamon (1 g)

Step-by-Step Instructions:
1. **Mixing:** Stir honey and cinnamon into the Greek yogurt.
2. **Serving:** Enjoy immediately as a quick snack or dessert.

Macronutrients:
Calories: 120 kcal | Protein: 8g | Carbohydrates: 15g | Fiber: 0g | Sugars: 12g | Total Fat: 2g | Saturated Fat: 1g | Cholesterol: 5mg | Sodium: 50mg | Potassium: 150mg

Micronutrients:
Vitamin A: 0% Daily Value | Vitamin C: 0% Daily Value | Calcium: 15% Daily Value | Iron: 0% Daily Value

65. Edamame with Sea Salt

⏰ Prep.Time: 5 minutes
Cook Time: 5 minutes
Total Time: 10 minutes

🔧 **Equipment Needed:** Pot, strainer

💪 **Difficulty:** 1/5

🛒 **Ingredient List for 1 Serving:**
- 1/2 cup shelled edamame (120 ml, 70 g)
- 1/4 teaspoon sea salt (1 g)

🏆 **Step-by-Step Instructions:**
1. **Boiling Edamame:** Bring a pot of water to a boil. Add edamame and cook for 3-5 minutes. Drain.
2. **Seasoning:** Sprinkle with sea salt and serve warm or cold.

🍽 **Macronutrients:**

Calories: 100 kcal | Protein: 8g | Carbohydrates: 8g | Fiber: 4g | Sugars: 2g | Total Fat: 3g | Saturated Fat: 0.5g | Cholesterol: 0mg | Sodium: 250mg | Potassium: 300mg

🔬 **Micronutrients:**

Vitamin A: 2% Daily Value | Vitamin C: 8% Daily Value | Calcium: 4% Daily Value | Iron: 8% Daily Value

66. Whole Grain Crackers with Cottage Cheese

⏰ Prep.Time: 5 minutes
Total Time: 5 minutes

🔧 **Equipment Needed:** Plate

💪 **Difficulty:** 1/5

🛒 **Ingredient List for 1 Serving:**
- 6 whole grain crackers (30 g)
- 1/4 cup cottage cheese (60 ml, 60 g)

🏆 **Step-by-Step Instructions:**
1. **Serving:** Spread cottage cheese on whole grain crackers and enjoy immediately as a snack.

🍽 **Macronutrients:**

Calories: 200 kcal | Protein: 9g | Carbohydrates: 24g | Fiber: 4g | Sugars: 2g | Total Fat: 6g | Saturated Fat: 2g | Cholesterol: 10mg | Sodium: 250mg | Potassium: 100mg

🔬 **Micronutrients:**

Vitamin A: 4% Daily Value | Vitamin C: 0% Daily Value | Calcium: 6% Daily Value | Iron: 6% Daily Value

67. Kale Chips Baked with Olive Oil and Sea Salt

Prep.Time: 5 minutes
Cook Time: 10 minutes
Total Time: 15 minutes

Equipment Needed: Baking sheet, oven

Difficulty: 2/5

Ingredient List for 1 Serving:
- 2 cups fresh kale, torn into pieces (480 ml, 60 g)
- 1 tablespoon olive oil (15 ml)
- 1/4 teaspoon sea salt (1 g)

Step-by-Step Instructions:
1. **Prepping Kale:** Preheat the oven to 350°F (180°C). Toss kale pieces with olive oil and sea salt.
2. **Baking:** Spread the kale on a baking sheet and bake for 10 minutes or until crispy.
3. **Serving:** Serve as a crunchy snack.

Macronutrients:
Calories: 150 kcal | Protein: 3g | Carbohydrates: 8g | Fiber: 4g | Sugars: 1g | Total Fat: 10g | Saturated Fat: 1.5g | Cholesterol: 0mg | Sodium: 250mg | Potassium: 400mg

Micronutrients:
Vitamin A: 200% Daily Value | Vitamin C: 100% Daily Value | Calcium: 10% Daily Value | Iron: 10% Daily Value

68. Cucumber and Tomato Salad with Feta Cheese

Prep.Time: 5 minutes
Total Time: 5 minutes

Equipment Needed: Mixing bowl

Difficulty: 1/5

Ingredient List for 1 Serving:
- 1/2 cup diced cucumber (120 ml, 60 g)
- 1/2 cup cherry tomatoes, halved (120 ml, 75 g)
- 2 tablespoons crumbled feta cheese (30 ml, 15 g)
- 1 tablespoon olive oil (15 ml)
- 1 teaspoon lemon juice (5 ml)

Step-by-Step Instructions:
1. **Mixing Salad:** Combine cucumber, tomatoes, and feta cheese in a mixing bowl.
2. **Dressing:** Drizzle with olive oil and lemon juice, and toss to coat.
3. **Serving:** Serve immediately.

Macronutrients:
Calories: 100 kcal | Protein: 3g | Carbohydrates: 6g | Fiber: 2g | Sugars: 3g | Total Fat: 8g | Saturated Fat: 3g | Cholesterol: 10mg | Sodium: 200mg | Potassium: 250mg

Micronutrients:
Vitamin A: 8% Daily Value | Vitamin C: 20% Daily Value | Calcium: 6% Daily Value | Iron: 4% Daily Value

69. Avocado Chocolate Mousse

⏰ **Prep. Time:** 10 minutes
Total Time: 10 minutes

🔧 **Equipment Needed:** Blender

💪 **Difficulty:** 2/5

🛒 **Ingredient List for 1 Serving:**
- 1/2 ripe avocado (about 75 g)
- 1 tablespoon cocoa powder (15 ml)
- 1 tablespoon honey (15 ml)
- 1/4 teaspoon vanilla extract (1 ml)

🍽 **Step-by-Step Instructions:**
1. **Blending:** Blend the avocado, cocoa powder, honey, and vanilla extract until smooth and creamy.
2. **Serving:** Serve chilled as a rich, healthy dessert.

🍴 **Macronutrients:**

Calories: 300 kcal | Protein: 3g | Carbohydrates: 35g | Fiber: 8g | Sugars: 25g | Total Fat: 18g | Saturated Fat: 2.5g | Cholesterol: 0mg | Sodium: 10mg | Potassium: 450mg

🔬 **Micronutrients:**

Vitamin A: 2% Daily Value | Vitamin C: 10% Daily Value | Calcium: 4% Daily Value | Iron: 10% Daily Value

70. Roasted Chickpeas with Smoked Paprika

⏰ **Prep. Time:** 5 minutes
Cook Time: 25 minutes
Total Time: 30 minutes

🔧 **Equipment Needed:** Baking sheet, oven

💪 **Difficulty:** 2/5

🛒 **Ingredient List for 1 Serving:**
- 1/2 cup cooked chickpeas (120 ml, 80 g)
- 1 tablespoon olive oil (15 ml)
- 1/2 teaspoon smoked paprika (2.5 g)
- Salt to taste

🍽 **Step-by-Step Instructions:**
1. **Prepping Chickpeas:** Preheat oven to 400°F (200°C). Toss chickpeas with olive oil, smoked paprika, and salt.
2. **Roasting:** Spread chickpeas on a baking sheet and roast for 25 minutes until crispy, stirring halfway through.
3. **Serving:** Serve warm as a crunchy snack.

🍴 **Macronutrients:**

Calories: 130 kcal | Protein: 5g | Carbohydrates: 15g | Fiber: 5g | Sugars: 1g | Total Fat: 6g | Saturated Fat: 1g | Cholesterol: 0mg | Sodium: 180mg | Potassium: 300mg

🔬 **Micronutrients:**

Vitamin A: 10% Daily Value | Vitamin C: 2% Daily Value | Calcium: 4% Daily Value | Iron: 8% Daily Value

71. Flaxseed Crackers with Guacamole

Prep.Time: 10 minutes
Total Time: 10 minutes

Equipment Needed: Mixing bowl

Difficulty: 2/5

Ingredient List for 1 Serving:
- 6 flaxseed crackers (30 g)
- 1/4 avocado, mashed (about 50 g)
- 1 teaspoon lemon juice (5 ml)
- Salt to taste

Step-by-Step Instructions:
1. **Making Guacamole:** In a small bowl, mash the avocado with lemon juice and salt.
2. **Serving:** Serve the guacamole with flaxseed crackers for dipping.

Macronutrients:
Calories: 180 kcal | Protein: 4g | Carbohydrates: 15g | Fiber: 6g | Sugars: 1g | Total Fat: 12g | Saturated Fat: 1.5g | Cholesterol: 0mg | Sodium: 150mg | Potassium: 350mg

Micronutrients:
Vitamin A: 2% Daily Value | Vitamin C: 8% Daily Value | Calcium: 4% Daily Value | Iron: 6% Daily Value

72. Mozzarella and Cherry Tomato Bites with Basil

Prep.Time: 5 minutes
Total Time: 5 minutes

Equipment Needed: Skewers

Difficulty: 1/5

Ingredient List for 1 Serving:
- 4 small mozzarella balls (about 30 g)
- 4 cherry tomatoes
- 4 fresh basil leaves
- 1 tablespoon olive oil (15 ml)
- 1/2 teaspoon balsamic vinegar (2.5 ml)

Step-by-Step Instructions:
1. **Assembling Bites:** Skewer each mozzarella ball with a cherry tomato and a basil leaf.
2. **Drizzling:** Drizzle with olive oil and balsamic vinegar.
3. **Serving:** Serve immediately as a fresh snack or appetizer.

Macronutrients:
Calories: 150 kcal | Protein: 7g | Carbohydrates: 4g | Fiber: 1g | Sugars: 2g | Total Fat: 12g | Saturated Fat: 4g | Cholesterol: 15mg | Sodium: 150mg | Potassium: 200mg

Micronutrients:
Vitamin A: 8% Daily Value | Vitamin C: 10% Daily Value | Calcium: 10% Daily Value | Iron: 2% Daily Value

73. Herb and Olive Oil Popcorn

Prep. Time: 5 minutes
Cook Time: 15 minutes
Total Time: 20 minutes

Equipment Needed: Large pot with lid

Difficulty: 1/5

Ingredient List for 1 Serving:
- 1/4 cup popcorn kernels (60 ml, 40 g)
- 1 tablespoon olive oil (15 ml)
- 1/4 teaspoon dried rosemary or thyme (1 g)
- Salt to taste

Step-by-Step Instructions:
1. **Popping Popcorn:** Heat olive oil in a large pot over medium heat. Add popcorn kernels and cover with a lid. Shake the pot occasionally until the popping slows down.
2. **Seasoning:** Toss with dried herbs and salt.
3. **Serving:** Serve immediately as a light snack.

Macronutrients:
Calories: 100 kcal | Protein: 2g | Carbohydrates: 12g | Fiber: 3g | Sugars: 0g | Total Fat: 6g | Saturated Fat: 1g | Cholesterol: 0mg | Sodium: 180mg | Potassium: 60mg

Micronutrients:
Vitamin A: 0% Daily Value | Vitamin C: 0% Daily Value | Calcium: 0% Daily Value | Iron: 4% Daily Value

74. Seed and Nut Mix with Dark Chocolate

Prep. Time: 5 minutes
Total Time: 5 minutes

Equipment Needed: Bowl

Difficulty: 1/5

Ingredient List for 1 Serving:
- 2 tablespoons sunflower seeds (30 ml, 15 g)
- 2 tablespoons almonds (30 ml, 15 g)
- 1 tablespoon dark chocolate chips (15 ml, 10 g)

Step-by-Step Instructions:
1. **Mixing:** Combine sunflower seeds, almonds, and dark chocolate chips in a bowl.
2. **Serving:** Enjoy as a quick snack.

Macronutrients:
Calories: 200 kcal | Protein: 5g | Carbohydrates: 12g | Fiber: 3g | Sugars: 6g | Total Fat: 16g | Saturated Fat: 4g | Cholesterol: 0mg | Sodium: 0mg | Potassium: 200mg

Micronutrients:
Vitamin A: 0% Daily Value | Vitamin C: 0% Daily Value | Calcium: 4% Daily Value | Iron: 6% Daily Value

75. Homemade Granola Bar with Almonds

Prep.Time: 10 minutes
Cook Time: 15 minutes
Total Time: 25 minutes

Equipment Needed: Baking sheet, mixing bowl

Difficulty: 3/5

Ingredient List for 1 Serving:
- 1/2 cup rolled oats (120 ml, 45 g)
- 2 tablespoons honey (30 ml)
- 1/4 cup almonds, chopped (60 ml, 30 g)
- 1 tablespoon chia seeds (15 ml, 10 g)
- 1 tablespoon peanut butter (15 ml, 16 g)

Step-by-Step Instructions:
1. **Mixing Ingredients:** Preheat oven to 350°F (180°C). In a mixing bowl, combine oats, honey, almonds, chia seeds, and peanut butter.
2. **Baking:** Press the mixture into a greased baking sheet and bake for 12-15 minutes until golden.
3. **Serving:** Let cool and cut into bars.

Macronutrients:
Calories: 250 kcal | Protein: 8g | Carbohydrates: 35g | Fiber: 6g | Sugars: 15g | Total Fat: 12g | Saturated Fat: 2g | Cholesterol: 0mg | Sodium: 50mg | Potassium: 200mg

Micronutrients:
Vitamin A: 0% Daily Value | Vitamin C: 0% Daily Value | Calcium: 6% Daily Value | Iron: 8% Daily Value

76. Yogurt with Granola, Blueberries, and Flaxseeds

Prep.Time: 5 minutes
Total Time: 5 minutes

Equipment Needed: Bowl, spoon

Difficulty: 1/5

Ingredient List for 1 Serving:
- 1/2 cup Greek yogurt (120 ml, 125 g)
- 2 tablespoons granola (30 ml, 15 g)
- 1/4 cup fresh blueberries (60 ml, 40 g)
- 1 tablespoon flaxseeds (15 ml, 10 g)

Step-by-Step Instructions:
1. **Mixing:** In a bowl, layer the Greek yogurt, granola, blueberries, and flaxseeds.
2. **Serving:** Serve immediately as a refreshing snack or breakfast.

Macronutrients:
Calories: 220 kcal | Protein: 8g | Carbohydrates: 30g | Fiber: 6g | Sugars: 15g | Total Fat: 7g | Saturated Fat: 1.5g | Cholesterol: 5mg | Sodium: 60mg | Potassium: 250mg

Micronutrients:
Vitamin A: 2% Daily Value | Vitamin C: 10% Daily Value | Calcium: 10% Daily Value | Iron: 8% Daily Value

77. Beet Hummus with Raw Vegetables

⏰ Prep. Time: 10 minutes
Cook Time: 15 minutes
Total Time: 25 minutes

🛠 **Equipment Needed:** Blender, mixing bowl

💪 **Difficulty:** 2/5

🛒 **Ingredient List for 2 Servings:**
- 1 small beet, roasted (about 60 g)
- 1/4 cup cooked chickpeas (60 ml, 40 g)
- 1 tablespoon tahini (15 ml)
- 1 tablespoon olive oil (15 ml)
- 1 teaspoon lemon juice (5 ml)
- 1 small carrot, sliced (about 60 g)
- 1 small cucumber, sliced (about 60 g)

🏆 **Step-by-Step Instructions:**
1. **Making Hummus:** Blend roasted beet, chickpeas, tahini, olive oil, and lemon juice in a blender until smooth.
2. **Serving:** Serve beet hummus with raw carrot and cucumber slices for dipping.

🍽 **Macronutrients:**
Calories: 160 kcal | Protein: 4g | Carbohydrates: 18g | Fiber: 6g | Sugars: 7g | Total Fat: 9g | Saturated Fat: 1g | Cholesterol: 0mg | Sodium: 160mg | Potassium: 400mg

🔬 **Micronutrients:**
Vitamin A: 100% Daily Value | Vitamin C: 10% Daily Value | Calcium: 6% Daily Value | Iron: 8% Daily Value

78. Oatmeal and Raisin Whole Grain Cookies

⏰ Prep. Time: 10 minutes
Cook Time: 12 minutes
Total Time: 22 minutes

🛠 **Equipment Needed:** Mixing bowl, baking sheet

💪 **Difficulty:** 2/5

🛒 **Ingredient List for 1 Serving (Makes 2-3 Cookies):**
- 1/4 cup rolled oats (60 ml, 20 g)
- 1/4 cup whole wheat flour (60 ml, 30 g)
- 1 tablespoon raisins (15 ml, 10 g)
- 1 tablespoon honey (15 ml)
- 1 tablespoon olive oil (15 ml)
- 1/2 teaspoon cinnamon (2.5 ml)

🏆 **Step-by-Step Instructions:**
1. **Mixing Dough:** Preheat the oven to 350°F (180°C). In a mixing bowl, combine oats, flour, raisins, honey, olive oil, and cinnamon.
2. **Baking:** Scoop the dough into cookie-sized portions and place on a baking sheet. Bake for 10-12 minutes until golden.
3. **Serving:** Let cool and enjoy.

🍽 **Macronutrients:**
Calories: 180 kcal | Protein: 4g | Carbohydrates: 30g | Fiber: 4g | Sugars: 12g | Total Fat: 6g | Saturated Fat: 1g | Cholesterol: 0mg | Sodium: 30mg | Potassium: 150mg

🔬 **Micronutrients:**
Vitamin A: 0% Daily Value | Vitamin C: 0% Daily Value | Calcium: 2% Daily Value | Iron: 6% Daily Value

79. Banana and Blueberry Ice Cream (Dairy-Free)

Prep.Time: 5 minutes
Freeze Time: 2 hours
Total Time: 2 hours 5 minutes

Equipment Needed: Blender, freezer

Difficulty: 2/5

Ingredient List for 1 Serving:
- 2 bananas, sliced and frozen (about 240 g)
- 1/2 cup blueberries, frozen (120 ml, 75 g)

Step-by-Step Instructions:
1. **Blending:** In a blender, blend frozen bananas and blueberries until smooth and creamy.
2. **Serving:** Serve immediately as soft serve or freeze for 1-2 hours for firmer texture.

Macronutrients:
Calories: 150 kcal | Protein: 2g | Carbohydrates: 35g | Fiber: 5g | Sugars: 25g | Total Fat: 0g | Saturated Fat: 0g | Cholesterol: 0mg | Sodium: 0mg | Potassium: 400mg

Micronutrients:
Vitamin A: 0% Daily Value | Vitamin C: 15% Daily Value | Calcium: 0% Daily Value | Iron: 2% Daily Value

80. Fruit Salad with Lime and Mint

Prep.Time: 5 minutes
Total Time: 5 minutes

Equipment Needed: Mixing bowl

Difficulty: 1/5

Ingredient List for 1 Serving:
- 1/2 cup diced pineapple (120 ml, 75 g)
- 1/2 cup diced watermelon (120 ml, 75 g)
- 1/2 cup diced mango (120 ml, 75 g)
- 1 teaspoon lime juice (5 ml)
- 1 tablespoon chopped fresh mint (15 ml)

Step-by-Step Instructions:
1. **Mixing:** Combine pineapple, watermelon, and mango in a bowl.
2. **Dressing:** Drizzle with lime juice and sprinkle with mint.
3. **Serving:** Serve immediately.

Macronutrients:
Calories: 100 kcal | Protein: 1g | Carbohydrates: 25g | Fiber: 3g | Sugars: 22g | Total Fat: 0g | Saturated Fat: 0g | Cholesterol: 0mg | Sodium: 5mg | Potassium: 250mg

Micronutrients:
Vitamin A: 25% Daily Value | Vitamin C: 80% Daily Value | Calcium: 2% Daily Value | Iron: 2% Daily Value

3.5 Desserts

81. Baked Apples with Cinnamon and Nutmeg

Prep. Time: 5 minutes
Cook Time: 20 minutes
Total Time: 25 minutes

Equipment Needed: Baking dish, oven

Difficulty: 2/5

Ingredient List for 1 Serving:
- 2 medium apples, cored (about 180 g each)
- 1 tablespoon honey (15 ml)
- 1/4 teaspoon ground cinnamon (1 g)
- 1/8 teaspoon ground nutmeg (0.5 g)

Step-by-Step Instructions:
1. **Prepping Apples:** Preheat the oven to 350°F (180°C). Place the cored apples in a baking dish.
2. **Adding Toppings:** Drizzle each apple with honey and sprinkle with cinnamon and nutmeg.
3. **Baking:** Bake for 20 minutes until soft and tender.
4. **Serving:** Serve warm.

Macronutrients:

Calories: 150 kcal | Protein: 0g | Carbohydrates: 40g | Fiber: 5g | Sugars: 35g | Total Fat: 0g | Saturated Fat: 0g | Cholesterol: 0mg | Sodium: 0mg | Potassium: 250mg

Micronutrients:

Vitamin A: 2% Daily Value | Vitamin C: 8% Daily Value | Calcium: 2% Daily Value | Iron: 2% Daily Value

82. Dark Chocolate and Almond Clusters

Prep. Time: 5 minutes
Freeze Time: 15 minutes
Total Time: 20 minutes

Equipment Needed: Baking sheet, freezer

Difficulty: 2/5

Ingredient List for 1 Serving:
- 1/4 cup dark chocolate chips (60 ml, 30 g)
- 1/4 cup almonds (60 ml, 30 g)

Step-by-Step Instructions:
1. **Melting Chocolate:** Melt the dark chocolate in the microwave or using a double boiler.
2. **Mixing:** Stir in the almonds until well-coated.
3. **Setting:** Drop spoonfuls of the mixture onto a baking sheet lined with parchment paper. Freeze for 15 minutes until firm.
4. **Serving:** Enjoy as a quick dessert or snack.

Macronutrients:

Calories: 220 kcal | Protein: 4g | Carbohydrates: 20g | Fiber: 5g | Sugars: 12g | Total Fat: 15g | Saturated Fat: 5g | Cholesterol: 0mg | Sodium: 0mg | Potassium: 250mg

Micronutrients:

Vitamin A: 0% Daily Value | Vitamin C: 0% Daily Value | Calcium: 6% Daily Value | Iron: 10% Daily Value

83. Berry Sorbet with Fresh Mint

Prep.Time: 10 minutes
Freeze Time: 2 hours
Total Time: 2 hours 10 minutes

Equipment Needed: Blender, freezer

Difficulty: 2/5

Ingredient List for 1 Serving:
- 1 cup mixed berries, frozen (240 ml, 150 g)
- 1 tablespoon honey (15 ml)
- 1 tablespoon lemon juice (15 ml)
- 1 teaspoon chopped fresh mint (5 ml)

Step-by-Step Instructions:
1. **Blending:** Blend the frozen berries, honey, lemon juice, and mint until smooth.
2. **Freezing:** Pour the mixture into a container and freeze for 2 hours, stirring occasionally.
3. **Serving:** Serve as a refreshing dessert.

Macronutrients:
Calories: 120 kcal | Protein: 1g | Carbohydrates: 30g | Fiber: 6g | Sugars: 24g | Total Fat: 0g | Saturated Fat: 0g | Cholesterol: 0mg | Sodium: 0mg | Potassium: 200mg

Micronutrients:
Vitamin A: 0% Daily Value | Vitamin C: 70% Daily Value | Calcium: 2% Daily Value | Iron: 4% Daily Value

84. Peach and Blueberry Crisp with Oats

Prep.Time: 10 minutes
Cook Time: 25 minutes
Total Time: 35 minutes

Equipment Needed: Baking dish, oven

Difficulty: 3/5

Ingredient List for 1 Serving:
- 1 medium peach, sliced (about 100 g)
- 1/2 cup fresh blueberries (120 ml, 75 g)
- 1/4 cup rolled oats (60 ml, 20 g)
- 1 tablespoon honey (15 ml)
- 1 tablespoon olive oil (15 ml)
- 1/2 teaspoon cinnamon (2.5 g)

Step-by-Step Instructions:
1. **Prepping Fruit:** Preheat the oven to 350°F (180°C). Arrange peach slices and blueberries in a baking dish.
2. **Making Topping:** In a bowl, mix rolled oats, honey, olive oil, and cinnamon. Sprinkle the mixture over the fruit.
3. **Baking:** Bake for 25 minutes until the topping is golden and the fruit is bubbly.
4. **Serving:** Serve warm as a healthy dessert.

Macronutrients:
Calories: 250 kcal | Protein: 3g | Carbohydrates: 45g | Fiber: 5g | Sugars: 25g | Total Fat: 8g | Saturated Fat: 1g | Cholesterol: 0mg | Sodium: 0mg | Potassium: 300mg

Micronutrients:
Vitamin A: 4% Daily Value | Vitamin C: 15% Daily Value | Calcium: 2% Daily Value | Iron: 6% Daily Value

85. Carrot Cake with Greek Yogurt Frosting

Prep. Time: 15 minutes
Cook Time: 25 minutes
Total Time: 40 minutes

Equipment Needed: Mixing bowl, baking dish

Difficulty: 3/5

Ingredient List for 1 Serving:
- 1/2 cup grated carrots (120 ml, 60 g)
- 1/4 cup whole wheat flour (60 ml, 30 g)
- 1 tablespoon honey (15 ml)
- 1 tablespoon olive oil (15 ml)
- 1/2 teaspoon cinnamon (2.5 ml)
- 1/4 cup Greek yogurt (60 ml, 60 g)
- 1 teaspoon lemon juice (5 ml)

Step-by-Step Instructions:
1. **Making Cake Batter:** Preheat oven to 350°F (180°C). In a bowl, mix grated carrots, whole wheat flour, honey, olive oil, and cinnamon. Pour into a greased baking dish.
2. **Baking:** Bake for 25 minutes or until a toothpick comes out clean.
3. **Making Frosting:** Mix Greek yogurt and lemon juice.
4. **Serving:** Let the cake cool, then top with the Greek yogurt frosting.

Macronutrients:
Calories: 280 kcal | Protein: 6g | Carbohydrates: 40g | Fiber: 5g | Sugars: 25g | Total Fat: 10g | Saturated Fat: 2g | Cholesterol: 0mg | Sodium: 100mg | Potassium: 300mg

Micronutrients:
Vitamin A: 100% Daily Value | Vitamin C: 10% Daily Value | Calcium: 10% Daily Value | Iron: 8% Daily Value

86. Banana and Walnut Ice Cream (Dairy-Free)

Prep. Time: 5 minutes
Freeze Time: 2 hours
Total Time: 2 hours 5 minutes

Equipment Needed: Blender, freezer

Difficulty: 2/5

Ingredient List for 1 Serving:
- 2 ripe bananas, sliced and frozen (about 240 g)
- 2 tablespoons chopped walnuts (30 ml, 15 g)

Step-by-Step Instructions:
1. **Blending:** In a blender, blend frozen banana slices until smooth.
2. **Mixing:** Stir in chopped walnuts.
3. **Freezing:** Freeze for 1-2 hours or until firm.
4. **Serving:** Serve as a dairy-free ice cream alternative.

Macronutrients:
Calories: 200 kcal | Protein: 3g | Carbohydrates: 35g | Fiber: 5g | Sugars: 25g | Total Fat: 6g | Saturated Fat: 0.5g | Cholesterol: 0mg | Sodium: 0mg | Potassium: 400mg

Micronutrients:
Vitamin A: 0% Daily Value | Vitamin C: 15% Daily Value | Calcium: 2% Daily Value | Iron: 2% Daily Value

87. Coconut and Chia Seed Pudding

Prep. Time: 5 minutes
Chill Time: 2 hours
Total Time: 2 hours 5 minutes

Equipment Needed: Mixing bowl, refrigerator

Difficulty: 2/5

Ingredient List for 1 Serving:
- 1/2 cup unsweetened coconut milk (120 ml)
- 2 tablespoons chia seeds (30 ml, 20 g)
- 1 tablespoon honey (15 ml)

Step-by-Step Instructions:
1. **Mixing:** In a bowl, combine coconut milk, chia seeds, and honey. Stir well.
2. **Chilling:** Refrigerate for at least 2 hours, stirring occasionally, until the mixture thickens.
3. **Serving:** Serve cold as a healthy pudding.

Macronutrients:
Calories: 180 kcal | Protein: 4g | Carbohydrates: 20g | Fiber: 8g | Sugars: 10g | Total Fat: 10g | Saturated Fat: 6g | Cholesterol: 0mg | Sodium: 10mg | Potassium: 150mg

Micronutrients:
Vitamin A: 0% Daily Value | Vitamin C: 0% Daily Value | Calcium: 15% Daily Value | Iron: 8% Daily Value

88. Almond Flour Lemon Bars

Prep. Time: 10 minutes
Cook Time: 25 minutes
Total Time: 35 minutes

Equipment Needed: Baking dish, mixing bowl

Difficulty: 3/5

Ingredient List for 1 Serving:
- 1/2 cup almond flour (120 ml, 50 g)
- 1 tablespoon honey (15 ml)
- 1 tablespoon lemon juice (15 ml)
- 1 large egg

Step-by-Step Instructions:
1. **Mixing Batter:** Preheat the oven to 350°F (180°C). In a bowl, mix almond flour, honey, lemon juice, and the egg until smooth.
2. **Baking:** Pour the mixture into a greased baking dish and bake for 20-25 minutes until firm.
3. **Serving:** Let cool before cutting into bars.

Macronutrients:
Calories: 150 kcal | Protein: 5g | Carbohydrates: 15g | Fiber: 3g | Sugars: 10g | Total Fat: 8g | Saturated Fat: 1g | Cholesterol: 45mg | Sodium: 40mg | Potassium: 60mg

Micronutrients:
Vitamin A: 2% Daily Value | Vitamin C: 8% Daily Value | Calcium: 4% Daily Value | Iron: 4% Daily Value

89. Chocolate Avocado Pudding

Prep. Time: 5 minutes
Total Time: 5 minutes

Equipment Needed: Blender

Difficulty: 2/5

Ingredient List for 1 Serving:
- 1/2 ripe avocado (about 75 g)
- 1 tablespoon cocoa powder (15 ml)
- 1 tablespoon honey (15 ml)
- 1/4 teaspoon vanilla extract (1 ml)

Step-by-Step Instructions:
1. **Blending:** Blend the avocado, cocoa powder, honey, and vanilla extract until smooth and creamy.
2. **Serving:** Serve chilled as a quick dessert.

Macronutrients:
Calories: 240 kcal | Protein: 3g | Carbohydrates: 25g | Fiber: 8g | Sugars: 20g | Total Fat: 15g | Saturated Fat: 2.5g | Cholesterol: 0mg | Sodium: 10mg | Potassium: 400mg

Micronutrients:
Vitamin A: 2% Daily Value | Vitamin C: 10% Daily Value | Calcium: 4% Daily Value | Iron: 10% Daily Value

90. Raspberry and Lemon Cheesecake (No-Bake)

Prep. Time: 15 minutes
Chill Time: 1 hour
Total Time: 1 hour 15 minutes

Equipment Needed: Mixing bowl, refrigerator

Difficulty: 3/5

Ingredient List for 1 Serving:
- 1/2 cup crushed graham crackers (120 ml, 40 g)
- 2 tablespoons melted butter (30 ml)
- 1/4 cup cream cheese (60 ml, 60 g)
- 1 tablespoon lemon juice (15 ml)
- 1/4 cup fresh raspberries (60 ml, 40 g)

Step-by-Step Instructions:
1. **Making Crust:** In a bowl, mix crushed graham crackers with melted butter. Press the mixture into the bottom of two small serving dishes.
2. **Making Filling:** In another bowl, combine cream cheese and lemon juice. Spread this mixture over the graham cracker crust.
3. **Chilling:** Chill in the refrigerator for at least 1 hour.
4. **Serving:** Top with fresh raspberries before serving.

Macronutrients:
Calories: 320 kcal | Protein: 4g | Carbohydrates: 25g | Fiber: 3g | Sugars: 15g | Total Fat: 22g | Saturated Fat: 12g | Cholesterol: 60mg | Sodium: 200mg | Potassium: 200mg

Micronutrients:
Vitamin A: 10% Daily Value | Vitamin C: 15% Daily Value | Calcium: 4% Daily Value | Iron: 4% Daily Value

91. Dark Chocolate and Walnut Brownies (Flourless)

Prep.Time: 10 minutes
Cook Time: 25 minutes
Total Time: 35 minutes

Equipment Needed: Baking dish, mixing bowl

Difficulty: 3/5

Ingredient List for 1 Serving:
- 1/4 cup dark chocolate chips (60 ml, 30 g)
- 2 tablespoons butter (30 ml, 30 g)
- 1/4 cup walnuts, chopped (60 ml, 30 g)
- 1 large egg
- 1 tablespoon cocoa powder (15 ml)
- 1 tablespoon honey (15 ml)

Step-by-Step Instructions:
1. **Melting Chocolate:** Preheat the oven to 350°F (180°C). Melt the dark chocolate and butter together in a microwave or double boiler.
2. **Mixing:** In a bowl, whisk the egg, then mix in cocoa powder, honey, and melted chocolate mixture. Stir in the chopped walnuts.
3. **Baking:** Pour the mixture into a greased baking dish and bake for 20-25 minutes.
4. **Serving:** Let cool before cutting into squares.

Macronutrients:
Calories: 220 kcal | Protein: 5g | Carbohydrates: 20g | Fiber: 3g | Sugars: 14g | Total Fat: 16g | Saturated Fat: 8g | Cholesterol: 60mg | Sodium: 50mg | Potassium: 250mg

Micronutrients:
Vitamin A: 4% Daily Value | Vitamin C: 0% Daily Value | Calcium: 4% Daily Value | Iron: 10% Daily Value

92. Avocado and Lime Ice Cream (Dairy-Free)

Prep.Time: 10 minutes
Freeze Time: 2 hours
Total Time: 2 hours 10 minutes

Equipment Needed: Blender, freezer

Difficulty: 2/5

Ingredient List for 1 Serving:
- 1 ripe avocado (about 150 g)
- 1 tablespoon lime juice (15 ml)
- 1 tablespoon honey (15 ml)
- 1/4 cup coconut milk (60 ml)

Step-by-Step Instructions:
1. **Blending:** Blend avocado, lime juice, honey, and coconut milk until smooth.
2. **Freezing:** Pour the mixture into a container and freeze for at least 2 hours, stirring occasionally.
3. **Serving:** Scoop and serve as a refreshing dairy-free dessert.

Macronutrients:
Calories: 170 kcal | Protein: 1g | Carbohydrates: 18g | Fiber: 5g | Sugars: 12g | Total Fat: 12g | Saturated Fat: 3g | Cholesterol: 0mg | Sodium: 5mg | Potassium: 400mg

Micronutrients:
Vitamin A: 2% Daily Value | Vitamin C: 15% Daily Value | Calcium: 2% Daily Value | Iron: 4% Daily Value

93. Whole Wheat Apple Cake with Cinnamon

Prep.Time: 15 minutes
Cook Time: 30 minutes
Total Time: 45 minutes

Equipment Needed: Baking dish, mixing bowl

Difficulty: 3/5

Ingredient List for 1 Serving:
- 1 small apple, peeled and diced (about 100 g)
- 1/4 cup whole wheat flour (60 ml, 30 g)
- 1 tablespoon honey (15 ml)
- 1/4 teaspoon cinnamon (1 g)
- 1/4 teaspoon baking powder (1 g)
- 1 large egg

Step-by-Step Instructions:
1. **Mixing Batter:** Preheat the oven to 350°F (180°C). In a bowl, mix whole wheat flour, cinnamon, baking powder, honey, and the egg. Fold in the diced apple.
2. **Baking:** Pour the batter into a greased baking dish and bake for 25-30 minutes until a toothpick comes out clean.
3. **Serving:** Let cool and serve warm or at room temperature.

Macronutrients:
Calories: 250 kcal | Protein: 6g | Carbohydrates: 40g | Fiber: 6g | Sugars: 20g | Total Fat: 8g | Saturated Fat: 1g | Cholesterol: 70mg | Sodium: 80mg | Potassium: 250mg

Micronutrients:
Vitamin A: 2% Daily Value | Vitamin C: 4% Daily Value | Calcium: 4% Daily Value | Iron: 8% Daily Value

94. Light Tiramisu with Greek Yogurt and Cocoa

Prep.Time: 10 minutes
Chill Time: 1 hour
Total Time: 1 hour 10 minutes

Equipment Needed: Mixing bowl, refrigerator

Difficulty: 3/5

Ingredient List for 1 Serving:
- 1/4 cup Greek yogurt (60 ml, 60 g)
- 1 tablespoon honey (15 ml)
- 1/2 teaspoon vanilla extract (2.5 ml)
- 4 ladyfingers
- 1 teaspoon cocoa powder (5 ml)
- 1/4 cup brewed coffee (60 ml)

Step-by-Step Instructions:
1. **Mixing Yogurt:** In a bowl, mix Greek yogurt, honey, and vanilla extract.
2. **Assembling:** Dip each ladyfinger in coffee and layer them in serving glasses. Spread the yogurt mixture on top.
3. **Finishing:** Dust with cocoa powder and chill for at least 1 hour.
4. **Serving:** Serve chilled as a light tiramisu.

Macronutrients:
Calories: 280 kcal | Protein: 6g | Carbohydrates: 45g | Fiber: 2g | Sugars: 30g | Total Fat: 6g | Saturated Fat: 3g | Cholesterol: 40mg | Sodium: 60mg | Potassium: 150mg

Micronutrients:
Vitamin A: 2% Daily Value | Vitamin C: 0% Daily Value | Calcium: 8% Daily Value | Iron: 4% Daily Value

95. Strawberry and Yogurt Mousse (Sugar-Free)

Prep.Time: 10 minutes
Chill Time: 1 hour
Total Time: 1 hour 10 minutes

Equipment Needed: Blender, refrigerator

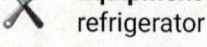

Difficulty: 2/5

Ingredient List for 1 Serving:
- 1/2 cup Greek yogurt (120 ml, 125 g)
- 1/2 cup fresh strawberries (120 ml, 75 g)
- 1 teaspoon honey (5 ml)

Step-by-Step Instructions:
1. **Blending:** Blend strawberries and honey until smooth. Gently fold the mixture into Greek yogurt.
2. **Chilling:** Refrigerate for at least 1 hour until firm.
3. **Serving:** Serve chilled as a light, sugar-free mousse.

Macronutrients:
Calories: 150 kcal | Protein: 8g | Carbohydrates: 20g | Fiber: 2g | Sugars: 15g | Total Fat: 4g | Saturated Fat: 1.5g | Cholesterol: 5mg | Sodium: 40mg | Potassium: 200mg

Micronutrients:
Vitamin A: 2% Daily Value | Vitamin C: 60% Daily Value | Calcium: 10% Daily Value | Iron: 2% Daily Value

96. Pumpkin Cheesecake with Nut Crust (No-Bake)

Prep.Time: 15 minutes
Chill Time: 2 hours
Total Time: 2 hours 15 minutes

Equipment Needed: Mixing bowl, refrigerator

Difficulty: 3/5

Ingredient List for 1 Serving:
- 1/4 cup almonds, crushed (60 ml, 30 g)
- 2 tablespoons butter, melted (30 ml)
- 1/4 cup pumpkin puree (60 ml, 60 g)
- 1/4 cup cream cheese (60 ml, 60 g)
- 1 tablespoon honey (15 ml)
- 1/4 teaspoon cinnamon (1 g)

Step-by-Step Instructions:
1. **Making Crust:** Mix crushed almonds and melted butter. Press into the bottom of two small serving dishes.
2. **Making Filling:** In a bowl, mix pumpkin puree, cream cheese, honey, and cinnamon. Spread this mixture over the almond crust.
3. **Chilling:** Refrigerate for at least 2 hours until firm.
4. **Serving:** Serve chilled as a no-bake pumpkin cheesecake.

Macronutrients:
Calories: 320 kcal | Protein: 6g | Carbohydrates: 25g | Fiber: 4g | Sugars: 20g | Total Fat: 22g | Saturated Fat: 10g | Cholesterol: 60mg | Sodium: 150mg | Potassium: 200mg

Micronutrients:
Vitamin A: 100% Daily Value | Vitamin C: 6% Daily Value | Calcium: 6% Daily Value | Iron: 8% Daily Value

3.6 Beverages

97. Green Tea with Lemon and Honey

Prep.Time: 2 minutes
Cook Time: 5 minutes
Total Time: 7 minutes

Equipment Needed: Teapot

Difficulty: 1/5

Ingredient List for 1 Serving:
- 1 green tea bag
- 1 cup boiling water (240 ml)
- 1 teaspoon honey (5 ml)
- 1 teaspoon lemon juice (5 ml)

Step-by-Step Instructions:
1. **Brewing Tea:** Steep the green tea bag in boiling water for 3-5 minutes.
2. **Adding Flavor:** Stir in honey and lemon juice.
3. **Serving:** Serve hot.

Macronutrients:

Calories: 40 kcal | Protein: 0g | Carbohydrates: 10g | Fiber: 0g | Sugars: 10g | Total Fat: 0g | Saturated Fat: 0g | Cholesterol: 0mg | Sodium: 0mg | Potassium: 20mg

Micronutrients:

Vitamin A: 0% Daily Value | Vitamin C: 2% Daily Value | Calcium: 0% Daily Value | Iron: 0% Daily Value

98. Beetroot and Ginger Juice

Prep.Time: 5 minutes
Total Time: 5 minutes

Equipment Needed: Juicer

Difficulty: 2/5

Ingredient List for 1 Serving:
- 1 small beetroot, peeled (about 100 g)
- 1 small apple (about 100 g)
- 1/2 inch piece of ginger, peeled (about 1 cm)

Step-by-Step Instructions:
1. **Juicing:** Juice the beetroot, apple, and ginger together in a juicer.
2. **Serving:** Serve immediately as a refreshing, nutrient-packed drink.

Macronutrients:

Calories: 110 kcal | Protein: 1g | Carbohydrates: 25g | Fiber: 4g | Sugars: 20g | Total Fat: 0g | Saturated Fat: 0g | Cholesterol: 0mg | Sodium: 70mg | Potassium: 300mg

Micronutrients:

Vitamin A: 2% Daily Value | Vitamin C: 15% Daily Value | Calcium: 2% Daily Value | Iron: 4% Daily Value

99. Turmeric and Pineapple Smoothie

Prep.Time: 5 minutes
Total Time: 5 minutes

Equipment Needed: Blender

Difficulty: 1/5

Ingredient List for 1 Serving:
- 1/2 cup fresh pineapple (120 ml, 75 g)
- 1/2 cup coconut water (120 ml)
- 1/2 teaspoon turmeric powder (2.5 g)
- 1 teaspoon honey (5 ml)

Step-by-Step Instructions:

1. **Blending:** Blend the pineapple, coconut water, turmeric, and honey until smooth.
2. **Serving:** Serve immediately as a refreshing and anti-inflammatory smoothie.

Macronutrients:

Calories: 150 kcal | Protein: 1g | Carbohydrates: 35g | Fiber: 4g | Sugars: 28g | Total Fat: 0g | Saturated Fat: 0g | Cholesterol: 0mg | Sodium: 60mg | Potassium: 250mg

Micronutrients:

Vitamin A: 2% Daily Value | Vitamin C: 100% Daily Value | Calcium: 2% Daily Value | Iron: 4% Daily Value

100. Cucumber Mint Water

Prep.Time: 5 minutes
Total Time: 5 minutes

Equipment Needed: Pitcher

Difficulty: 1/5

Ingredient List for 2 Servings:
- 1/2 cucumber, sliced (about 60 g)
- 5 fresh mint leaves
- 2 cups cold water (480 ml)

Step-by-Step Instructions:

1. **Infusing Water:** In a pitcher, combine cucumber slices, mint leaves, and cold water. Let sit for 5 minutes.
2. **Serving:** Serve chilled as a refreshing, hydrating drink.

Macronutrients:

Calories: 5 kcal | Protein: 0g | Carbohydrates: 1g | Fiber: 0g | Sugars: 0g | Total Fat: 0g | Saturated Fat: 0g | Cholesterol: 0mg | Sodium: 0mg | Potassium: 30mg

Micronutrients:

Vitamin A: 0% Daily Value | Vitamin C: 2% Daily Value | Calcium: 0% Daily Value | Iron: 0% Daily Value

101. Pomegranate and Lime Spritzer

Prep. Time: 5 minutes
Total Time: 5 minutes

Equipment Needed: Glass

Difficulty: 1/5

Ingredient List for 1 Serving:
- 1/4 cup pomegranate juice (60 ml)
- 1 teaspoon lime juice (5 ml)
- 1 cup sparkling water (240 ml)

Step-by-Step Instructions:
1. **Mixing:** In a glass, mix the pomegranate juice and lime juice.
2. **Adding Water:** Top with sparkling water.
3. **Serving:** Serve over ice for a refreshing, bubbly drink.

Macronutrients:
Calories: 120 kcal | Protein: 0g | Carbohydrates: 30g | Fiber: 0g | Sugars: 25g | Total Fat: 0g | Saturated Fat: 0g | Cholesterol: 0mg | Sodium: 10mg | Potassium: 200mg

Micronutrients:
Vitamin A: 0% Daily Value | Vitamin C: 10% Daily Value | Calcium: 2% Daily Value | Iron: 2% Daily Value

Elevate Your Heart Healthy Cookbook Journey with These Exclusive Bonuses

Access them directly with ease:

Bonus 1: 28-Day Fit Meal Plan

Jumpstart your heart-healthy journey with this carefully crafted 28-day meal plan. Packed with nutritious, easy-to-follow recipes, it's designed to boost your energy, support your heart health, and keep you on track with delicious, balanced meals every day.

SCAN this QR code:

Bonus 2: Weekly Meal Planner

Easily track what you eat each day with this simple Weekly Meal Planner. It's designed to help you stay organized and focused on your heart-healthy journey, making it easy to monitor your meals and stay on course.

SCAN this QR code:

Bonus 3: 30 Heart Healthy Smoothies

Add variety and flavor to your diet with these 30 delicious, heart-boosting smoothies. Each recipe is packed with ingredients known to support cardiovascular health, offering a quick and tasty way to nourish your body any time of the day.

SCAN this QR code:

Bonus 4: 10 Mindfulness Exercises

Support your heart health beyond the kitchen with these 10 simple mindfulness exercises. Designed to reduce stress and promote mental well-being, these practices are the perfect complement to your healthy eating habits, helping you maintain a balanced lifestyle.

SCAN this QR code:

YOUR OPINION MATTERS!

Leave your HONEST REVIEW

to GREATLY support my path as an author.

Thank YOU so much!

CHAPTER 4: STAYING COMMITTED TO HEART HEALTH

Achieving and maintaining heart health is a long-term commitment. While it may seem daunting to sustain healthy habits over time, the key is to make small, gradual changes that fit naturally into your daily life. This chapter will guide you through strategies to stay motivated, track your progress, and inspire others along the way.

4.1 Maintaining Long-Term Motivation

One of the biggest challenges in heart health is maintaining consistency in your lifestyle changes. Whether it's following a balanced diet or making time for regular exercise, the key to success is keeping motivation alive over the long term.

Creating Healthy Eating Habits That Stick

The foundation of lasting heart health lies in creating habits that are sustainable. Here are some practical tips to help you develop eating habits that will stay with you for life:

- **Start Small**: Focus on one change at a time, such as replacing refined grains with whole grains or incorporating more vegetables into your meals. Once a small change becomes routine, add another.

- **Make Meal Prep a Habit**: Preparing meals in advance helps avoid the temptation to grab fast food or convenience meals when you're short on time. Batch cooking or preparing snacks ahead of time ensures that healthy options are always available.

- **Incorporate a Variety of Foods**: A diverse diet not only ensures that you get all the necessary nutrients but also keeps your meals interesting. Rotate through different vegetables, whole grains, and proteins to prevent monotony.

- **Mindful Eating**: Pay attention to your hunger and fullness cues. Eating slowly and savoring your food can help you avoid overeating and make healthier choices more satisfying.

Overcoming the Temptation of Fast Food and Convenience Meals

Fast food and convenience meals are often filled with unhealthy fats, refined carbohydrates, and excessive sodium—all detrimental to heart health. However, they can be tempting due to their convenience. Here's how to overcome the urge:

- **Prepare Quick Alternatives**: Keep easy-to-make, heart-healthy meals on hand, like salads, whole-grain sandwiches, or vegetable stir-fries. Having ready-made healthy snacks like nuts or fruit also helps curb cravings.

- **Plan Your Meals**: Weekly meal planning can save you time and help you avoid impulsive decisions. Designate a specific day to plan your meals and prepare a grocery list, focusing on whole foods and fresh ingredients.

- **Healthier Versions of Favorite Meals**: Recreate your favorite fast food meals in healthier ways at home. For example, make baked sweet potato fries instead of regular fries, or a homemade turkey burger on whole wheat bread.

- **Stay Hydrated**: Often, thirst can be mistaken for hunger. Drink water throughout the day to stay hydrated and prevent unnecessary snacking.

How to Keep Cooking Fun and Enjoyable

Cooking can feel like a chore if it's always rushed or repetitive. To stay excited about preparing healthy meals, it's important to bring creativity and enjoyment into the kitchen.

- **Experiment with New Recipes**: Regularly try out new recipes that challenge your skills or introduce you to new ingredients. This can make cooking more adventurous and rewarding.

- **Involve Your Family**: Cooking with your spouse or children can be a bonding experience and make the process more enjoyable. Involving them in meal planning can also help cater meals to everyone's preferences.

- **Use Music or Podcasts**: Listening to music or podcasts while cooking can make the process more relaxing and enjoyable.

- **Presentation Matters**: Taking time to present your meals nicely, even if you're eating alone, can elevate the experience. A beautifully plated dish feels more rewarding to eat.

4.2 Tracking Your Progress

Staying on track with your heart health goals requires monitoring your progress. Consistent tracking helps you identify areas of improvement, celebrate your successes, and stay motivated for the long haul.

How to Monitor Heart Health with Your Diet

Diet plays a critical role in managing heart health. Monitoring your intake helps ensure you're consuming the right nutrients while staying within your calorie goals. Here's how to keep an eye on your dietary impact:

- **Track Nutrients**: Focus on monitoring key nutrients that affect heart health, such as fiber, sodium, saturated fats, and cholesterol. Aim to reduce sodium and saturated fat intake while increasing fiber-rich foods like vegetables, whole grains, and legumes.

- **Keep a Food Journal**: Write down everything you eat, including portion sizes and times of meals. This can reveal patterns you might not be aware of, like mindless snacking or skipping meals.

- **Consult a Professional**: If possible, work with a dietitian to review your progress and make adjustments as needed. They can help ensure that your diet is balanced and tailored to your specific needs.

Celebrating Small Wins and Staying Inspired

Achieving long-term heart health is a journey that requires persistence and positivity. Celebrating small wins along the way can keep you motivated:

- **Set Realistic Goals**: Break down your overall health goals into smaller, achievable milestones, such as reducing cholesterol by a certain number of points or integrating vegetables into one meal per day.
- **Reward Yourself**: Non-food-related rewards can provide additional motivation. For example, treat yourself to a new workout outfit or a relaxing massage when you hit a goal.
- **Document Your Journey**: Take photos of your meals, workouts, or even your physical progress. Documenting your journey visually can serve as a reminder of how far you've come.

Using Meal Logs and Nutritional Apps for Consistency

Meal logging apps and fitness trackers have become valuable tools for staying consistent in your heart health journey:

- **Choose a User-Friendly App**: Use apps like MyFitnessPal, Cronometer, or Yazio that allow you to log meals, scan barcodes, and track macros like protein, fats, and fiber. These apps can also help track sodium and sugar intake, which are critical for heart health.
- **Set Notifications**: Most apps allow you to set reminders to log meals or drink water, ensuring that you stay on track throughout the day.
- **Analyze Your Trends**: After a few weeks of tracking, review your intake trends. Are you consistently meeting your fiber goals? Are you eating too much sugar? Use this data to make small but impactful changes.

4.3 Inspiring Heart-Healthy Habits in Others

Encouraging others to adopt heart-healthy habits not only helps them but can also reinforce your own healthy lifestyle. By sharing knowledge and experiences, you can create a positive ripple effect in your community.

Sharing Recipes with Friends and Family

Sharing your favorite heart-healthy recipes is a great way to inspire others:

- **Host a Cooking Night**: Invite friends or family over for a heart-healthy meal. Teach them how to make a few simple, nutritious recipes they can take home.
- **Social Media Sharing**: Post your heart-healthy meals on social media with recipes and tips. This can inspire your network to try new healthy dishes.
- **Recipe Exchange**: Start a recipe exchange with friends or family, where each person contributes a favorite healthy recipe. This can give everyone new ideas and expand their meal repertoire.

Educating Others on Heart Health

Educating your community about the importance of heart health can have a lasting impact. Here's how you can lead by example:

- **Lead by Example**: The best way to inspire others is by showing them the benefits of heart-healthy living in your own life. When they see your success and improvements, they may be motivated to follow.

- **Offer Support**: Be a source of support for friends or family who may be struggling with their own health goals. Encourage them with positivity and provide resources like articles, podcasts, or documentaries about heart health.

- **Join Heart-Healthy Initiatives**: Participate in community events, such as heart health awareness walks or local cooking classes focused on nutrition. This can help you meet like-minded individuals and contribute to a broader impact.

INGREDIENT INDEX

A
- apple 16, 41, 51, 57, 59
- avocado 11, 17, 22, 25, 26, 29, 37, 45, 46, 55, 56

B
- balsamic vinegar 23, 24, 29, 46
- banana 13, 14, 20, 53, 70
- basil leaves 40, 46
- bell peppers 28, 30, 32, 33, 34, 37, 39
- black beans 15, 25
- blueberries 20, 48, 50, 52
- broccoli 30, 31, 32, 37, 40
- brown rice 27, 32, 38

C
- carrots 22, 24, 27, 33, 36, 37, 53
- cauliflower 34
- chia seeds 12, 13, 17, 18, 20, 48, 54
- chickpeas 21, 27, 29, 45, 49
- chili powder 25
- cinnamon 12, 13, 14, 16, 42, 49, 51, 52, 53, 57, 58
- coconut milk 54, 56
- cucumber 21, 23, 26, 44, 49, 60

D
- dark chocolate 47, 51, 56

E
- eggplant 34, 38

F
- flaxseeds 14, 48

G
- garlic 35, 40
- ginger 24, 59
- Greek yogurt 15, 18, 21, 25, 26, 27, 40, 42, 48, 53, 57, 58

H
- honey 12, 13, 15, 16, 18, 42, 45, 48, 49, 51, 52, 53, 54, 55, 56, 57, 58, 59, 60

K
- kale 14, 22, 28, 44

L
- lemon 11, 20, 21, 23, 25, 26, 27, 28, 29, 30, 34, 36, 37, 39, 44, 46, 49, 52, 53, 54, 55, 59
- lentils 22, 33, 36
- lime 50, 56, 61

M
- mango 50
- maple syrup 12, 13, 16, 17
- mushrooms 14, 38

N

- nutmeg 51

O

- oats 12, 16, 48, 49, 52
- olive oil 11, 13, 14, 15, 17, 18, 19, 20, 21, 22, 23, 24, 25, 26, 27, 28, 29, 30, 31, 32, 33, 34, 35, 36, 37, 38, 39, 40, 44, 45, 46, 47, 49, 52, 53
- onion 25
- orange 28

P

- paprika 31, 45
- parsley 34
- peanut butter 48
- pineapple 50, 60
- potatoes 31, 36

Q

- quinoa 12, 21, 31, 34, 37

S

- Salt 11, 14, 15, 19, 21, 22, 25, 26, 27, 28, 29, 30, 31, 32, 33, 34, 35, 36, 37, 38, 39, 40, 43, 44, 45, 46, 47
- sesame seeds 39
- spinach 11, 17, 19, 23, 26, 30, 35, 36, 39
- strawberries 23, 58
- sweet potatoes 31, 36

T

- tofu 32, 37
- tomatoes 19, 21, 25, 26, 29, 32, 33, 34, 44, 46

V

- vanilla extract 12, 13, 45, 55, 57

W

- walnuts 13, 23, 53, 56

Z

- zucchini 27, 28, 30, 32, 33, 34

VEGAN SUBSTITUTES

Ingredient	Recipe Number(s)	Vegan Substitute
Bacon	(#26)	Tempeh bacon or coconut bacon
Beef	(#19, #20)	Seitan, lentils, or textured vegetable protein (TVP)
Cheese	(#17, #19, #29)	Vegan cheese or nutritional yeast
Chicken	(#21, #22, #23, #24, #25)	Tofu, tempeh, or seitan
Cottage Cheese	(#29, #30)	Silken tofu or cashew cream
Cream Cheese	(#28)	Cashew cream or vegan cream cheese
Eggs	(#16, #17, #18, #19)	Mashed banana, applesauce, or flaxseed meal
Greek Yogurt	(#19, #30, #30)	Coconut yogurt or soy yogurt
Honey	(potential use)	Maple syrup or agave nectar
Milk	(#15, #24, #27)	Almond milk, soy milk, or oat milk
Protein Pancakes	(#18)	Vegan protein powder and plant milk
Prawns	(#27)	Vegan prawns or marinated tofu
Salmon	(#22, #25)	Marinated tofu or chickpea fillets
Steak	(#21)	Portobello mushrooms or seitan steak
Shrimp	(#29, #29)	Vegan shrimp or marinated tofu
Tuna	(#21)	Chickpea mash or vegan tuna
Turkey	(#18, #23, #28)	Tempeh bacon or tofu slices
Turkey Sausage	(#18)	Soy sausage or tempeh sausage

BIO AUTHOR

Karen McBeal is a passionate nutritionist, culinary expert, and fitness enthusiast who is dedicated to helping people lead healthier, more balanced lives through nutritious food and active living. With a lifelong commitment to fitness, Karen has spent years refining her understanding of how a combination of regular exercise and wholesome eating can optimize overall health and well-being. This dual expertise in nutrition and fitness allows her to craft recipes that not only taste great but also fuel the body for peak performance.

After overcoming her own health challenges, Karen discovered the transformative power of food and fitness in achieving lasting wellness. Her specialty lies in creating easy-to-follow, low-carb, high-protein recipes that are both satisfying and packed with nutrients. Karen's philosophy is grounded in simplicity—she believes that anyone can enjoy a healthy lifestyle with the right tools and guidance, and her recipes reflect this by being accessible for busy individuals looking to maximize their health without sacrificing flavor or convenience.

As an experienced fitness practitioner, Karen integrates her passion for movement into her approach to healthy living, ensuring that her recipes support not only a balanced diet but also an active lifestyle. Whether it's through strength training, yoga, or hiking, she understands how proper nutrition complements physical activity to enhance energy levels, recovery, and overall vitality.

When she's not in the kitchen or working out, Karen enjoys practicing yoga, exploring the outdoors, and spending time with her family. Her mission is to inspire others to take control of their health through mindful eating and regular exercise, proving that healthy living is not just achievable but enjoyable. With every recipe and fitness tip, she empowers others to optimize their well-being, one meal and workout at a time.

YOUR OPINION MATTERS!

Leave your HONEST REVIEW

to GREATLY support my path as an author.

Thank YOU so much!